Cooper's Morning Inspirations:

Daily Scriptures

By Chaplain Cooper

Published by Salt Water Media
29 Broad Street, Suite 104
Berlin, MD 21811
www.saltwatermedia.com

Salt-Water
M E D I A

Unless otherwise indicated, Bible quotations are taken from the New International Version. Copyright © 2011 by Zondervan.

Cover image by unsplash.com user Aaron Burden. Author image courtesy of the author.

Previous (First Edition) printed under ISBN 9781626972483 by Xulon Press -- www.xulonpress.com

This book will challenge you to read the Bible more, search the scriptures, and seek God for yourself.

But seek first the kingdom of God
and His righteousness
and all these things will be added to you.
(Matthew 6: 33)

DEDICATION

This Book is dedicated to my children. *Cooper's Morning Inspirations: Daily Scriptures* is a revised version of my first book, *Cooper's Morning Inspirations: A Spiritual Journey.* A Spiritual Journey was written with the intentions that people would read the book and want to search the Bible to seek understanding for themselves. God inspired me to write A Spiritual Journey, so I could see my spiritual journey, as well as individuals realizing their own spiritual journey by searching the Scriptures.

Cooper's Morning Inspirations: Daily Scriptures was revised to give it a new look and hopefully attract more people to want to read it. It is truly anointed, by God, since He is the Author, but used me to write the book. My hope is that everyone will take the time each day to talk with God. My prayer is that God will pour out His Spirit upon each person reading this book will be blessed, healed, set-free and delivered. With all my heart and soul, I dedicate this book to my Lord and savior, Jesus Christ., because with Him giving the strength and endurance I would never have finished it. "Amen!"

- Chaplain Cooper

Spiritual Journal

Today is December 31, at 8:00 a.m. I have decided to start writing a daily journal and morning inspirational manuscript. This book will allow me to keep track of all my personal thoughts on a daily basis. In early November, God laid in my heart to consider writing things down on paper. (Habakkuk 2:2 – Then the Lord answered me and said: "Write the vision and make it plain on tablets, that he may run who reads it.") Almost every morning at 6:00 a.m., I go to church and lie before God and pray. I shared these thoughts with my children, and my friends. I also have my very best friends from college on a mass-text list. I will send these text messages out immediately after leaving the sanctuary, so it will be a fresh word from the Lord. "I" thought to "myself" that "I" would wait until January to begin this process; because of school, work and just not knowing how or where to begin. I put ("I") and ("myself") in quotations, because God wanted to let me know; it's not about ("me"), but "Him." On December 1, I began writing morning inspirations to my children, and friends. I already had their names and phone numbers in my phone to send one text message to them all, at the same time. As I was writing, I kept thinking to myself, I should record them, because I got some positive responses from most of the children. I will mark today as the first day of recording my future book entitled, *Cooper's Morning Inspirations*. I called this book "Cooper's" Morning Inspirations, because I wanted to leave a legacy, of my name for future generations. I want the generations before and after me know that someone in the Cooper family was used by God to write a book. There will be another book coming soon to bookstores near you; and then others to follow.

DAY 1
(December 31)

"In the upcoming year will you stand for God? Will you (know) God or will you have (no) God?"

This message is to allow each of us to examine our lives as we begin to read these morning inspirations. Many times we say we are Christians and love God, but our lifestyle does not reflect it. Let's take time, from this day forth, to re-evaluate ourselves and start living and representing ourselves as Christians.

DAY 2
(January 1)

*Nahum 1:7

"The Lord is *good,* a stronghold in the day of trouble; and He knows them that trust Him."

"Happy New Year to my wife, my children and my grandchildren; I love you all very much".

I pray and ask God to help me write this book in order to prove my love towards Him and to keep seeking His face. I want to get closer to God and develop a personal (intimate) relationship with Him. God is my strength and my life. I will continue to minister to God's people for the rest of my life. Thank You, Lord for trusting me with this assignment.

DAY 3
(January 2)

*Romans 10: 1-5

"Brothers and sisters, my heart's desire and prayer to God is, that you might be saved . . . That the man which does those things shall live by them."

Don't just talk about it, be about it. Don't just talk the talk, but walk the walk. Be for-real with God and yourself.

DAY 4
(January 3)

*Psalm 100

"*Make a joyful noise unto the Lord. . .* Serve the Lord with gladness: come before His presence with singing. Know that the Lord, He is God: it is He that has made us, and not we ourselves; we are His people, and the sheep of His pasture. *Enter into His gates with thanksgiving, and into His courts with praise*: be thankful unto Him, and bless His name. For the Lord is good; His mercy is everlasting; and His truth endures to all generations."

Everything and everybody belong to God. He made the world in six days and rested on the seventh. Look at all His wonderful creations that are before our eyes. He is good; He is marvelous; He is wonderful, He is God. He is King of kings, Lord of lords; He is the first and the last. He is Alpha and Omega. He is a present help, always available when we need Him. Take time to give God your time on a daily basis. Come before Him with praise and thanksgiving. God is our Father who loves us very much.

$$\Omega A$$

DAY 5
(January 4)

Jeremiah 18: 1-6

"The word which came to Jeremiah from the Lord, saying *Arise, and go down to the potter's house* . . . and behold, he wrought a work on the wheels . . . Then the Lord came saying . . . cannot I do with you as this potter, said the Lord. Behold, *as the clay is in the potter's hand, so are you in my hand.*"

Today is the day that the Lord has made, let's rejoice and be glad in it. Let's ask God to make us over again. Renew the right spirit in us. Make us more like Him that we may dwell in the house of the Lord forever.

DAY 6
(January 5)

Romans 8:1-10

"There is therefore now no condemnation to them which are in Christ Jesus, who walk not in after the flesh, but after the Spirit. And if Christ be in you, the body is dead because of sin; but the Spirit is life because of righteousness."

Today, we have the opportunity to make a conscious decision to live right and walk right before God. Let's think, talk, and do things that are pleasing to God. Let's think about doing what is right to get into heaven. If we are pleasing to God, nothing can separate us from His love.

DAY 7
(January 6)

*James 3: 7-10

"For every kind of beasts, and of birds, and of serpents, and of things in the sea, is tamed, and have been tamed of mankind. *But the tongue can no man tame; it is an unruly evil, full of deadly poison* . . . Out of the same mouth proceeds blessing and cursing, these thing ought not to be."

Remember the saying, "Sticks and stones may break my bones, but names will never harm me." As I got older, I realized this statement is so false. Name calling will hurt you more and longer than sticks and stones. The pain from words can last for days, weeks, months, and even years. Let's pay attention to what we say about ourselves; as well as how we speak to others.

DAY 8
(January 7)

Ephesians 6: 10-20

"Finally, be strong in the Lord, and in the power of His might. *Put on the whole armor of God that you may be able to stand against the wiles of the devil.* For we wrestle not against flesh and blood, but against principalities, against powers, against the rulers of the darkness of this world, against spiritual wickedness in high places. Wherefore take unto you the whole armor of God, that you may be able to withstand in the evil day . . . having your loins girt about with truth, and having on the breastplate of righteousness; and your feet shod with the preparation of the gospel of peace . . . taking on the shield of faith; the helmet of salvation and the sword of the spirit, which is God."

There is a war going on in the spirit that is between good and evil; the devil and God. We, as children of God, must prepare ourselves to withstand attacks from the devil. Read the word of God; which is our sword. God is our strength and our salvation.

DAY 9
(January 8)

*Genesis 1: 1-2

"In the beginning God created the heaven and the earth." And the earth was without form, and void; and darkness was upon the face of the deep. And the Spirit of God moved upon the face of the waters."

In the beginning there was God. God created the heavens and the earth. The earth was without form, and there was no human life here. Because of God we exist today. Let's take the time to thank God for all He has done for us. Let us go into the house of the Lord and give Him the praise and honor He desires.

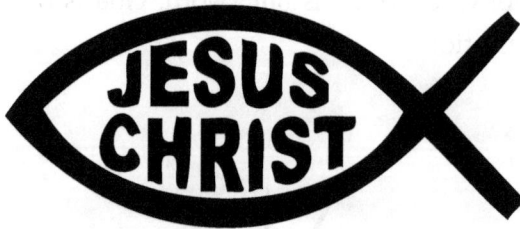

DAY 10
(January 9)

*Hebrews 11:1-6

"*Now faith is the substance of things hoped for, the evidence of things not seen.* Through faith we understand that the worlds were framed by the word of God, so that things which are seen were not made of things which do appear . . . But without faith it is impossible to please Him: for he that comes to God must believe that He is and that He rewards them that diligently seek Him."

We must have faith to please God. "God is Love" I believe we must start with loving one another and asking God to increase our faith. All good and perfect gifts come from the Lord. It is clearly a gift from God to be able to love all people. We must diligently seek Him. Pray daily for god-like love, and believe. "I love you, all!"

Prayer:

First, I want to give honor and praise to God, my Lord and Savior, Jesus Christ. I want to magnify His name and let Him know that I love Him very much; with my whole heart, mind, body, and soul. I pray for continual relationship with the One who saved me from the sins that I was bound by. Father, forgive me for anything and everything I have done against You. I repent, right now, and ask if You would give me another chance to serve and please You. Help me Lord. I love You Lord. This is my prayer, in Jesus' name, Amen, and Amen again. "Thank you, Jesus!"

I decided to write this prayer for a very special reason. First, I will share a few personal characteristics about myself. I am a very anxious person. I love to serve and help other people. I sometimes feel there is not enough time in a day to do all the things I have planned. I seem to always have to be doing something. I personally feel if I am not busy; the day is wasted.

Today, I sent the morning inspiration out to my wife, children, and best friends. At noontime today, no one had responded to the morning inspiration, except my wife True. Well, being that I was so anxious and excited about their comments, I could not take not hearing from them that late. I decided to send a mass-text to find out what was the delay. To my surprise, the children confirmed to me that they did not want me to stop sending the morning inspirations. Everyone had a legitimate excuse for the delay. This news brought tears to my eyes. I immediately asked God to forgive me for being so quick to rush His process. I have to remember, this is His book. God let me know today that I am just being used to write it. *Cooper's Morning Inspirations* is all about God.

DAY 11
(January 10)

Mark 11: 22-26

"And Jesus answered and said to them, have faith in God. For verily I say to you, that whoever shall say to this mountain, be removed, and be casted into the sea; and shall not doubt in his heart, but shall believe that those things which he says shall come to pass; he shall have whatsoever he says . . . And when you stand praying, forgive, that your Father also, which is in heaven may forgive you your trespasses. *But if you do not forgive, neither will your Father which is in heaven forgive your trespasses.*"

Have faith in God. Pray for everything, even to forgive our enemies. Whenever possible, ask for forgiveness from others, even if we are not the one who did the wrong. Forgiveness is pleasing to God. Ask God to bless us with a forgiving heart and to create in us a clean heart, forgiving others. This attitude will allow God to move mountains in our lives.

DAY 12
(January 11)

1 Peter 5: 5-7

"Likewise, you who are younger, submit yourselves to the elders. All of you be subject one to another, and be clothed with humility: for *God resists the proud, and gives grace to the humble.* Humble yourselves therefore under the mighty hand of God, that he may exalt you in due time: Casting all your care upon Him; for He cares for you."

Today's youths are becoming more disrespectful to the older generation. It is time, for the saints of God to take a stand together, and speak to our young men and women about the proper way to show respect. God's word is the same yesterday, today, and forevermore. It takes all of us to come together for the good of our young people. Let's pray that our children be humble to one another and cast their cares upon the Lord, to one day be exalted.

Exodus 20: 1-20

"And God spoke all these words, saying, I am the Lord your God, which have brought you out of the land of Egypt, out of the house of bondage. *You shall have no other gods before Me* ... And showing mercy unto thousands of them that love Me, and keep My commandment . . . And Moses said unto the people, Fear not: for God is come to prove you, and that his fear may be before your faces, that you sin not."

We serve a jealous God. We should only serve the one God; who is our Father, who art in heaven. He has laid out the Ten Commandments that He expects us to follow. It is up to us to pray to God and ask for help daily with these things. We must ask for forgiveness on a daily basis for sinning against God. He is our present help.

DAY 14:
(January 13)

Matthew 22: 37-39

"Jesus said unto him, *You shalt love the Lord your God with all your heart and with all your soul, and with all your mind.* This is the first and great commandment. And the second is like it: *Thou shalt love your neighbor as yourself.* On these two commandments hang all the prophets."

The Lord God wants us to love Him with everything that is within us. He knows our hearts. We should examine ourselves to see how serious we are in our relationship with the Lord. God is worth our very best. Let's give Him all of us. Keep your mind stayed on Jesus.

DAY 15:
(January 14)

Titus 3: 3-8

"*For we ourselves were sometimes foolish, disobedient, deceived, serving divers' lust and pleasures,* living in malice and envy, hateful, and hating one another. But after that the kindness and love of God our savior towards man appeared. Not by works of righteousness which we have done, but according to His mercy He saved us . . . made heirs according to the hope of eternal life . . . This is a faithful saying . . . These things are good and profitable unto men."

We are saved only by the grace and love of God. Good works are okay, but that's not what gets us into heaven. The grace and mercy of our heavenly Father adopted us into His kingdom. Let's continue to do good works, for the Lord that He will appear in our lives. His word is truth and is everlasting.

DAY 16:
(January 15)

3 John 2-8

"Beloved, I wish above all things that you may prosper and be in good health; even as your soul prospers . . . I have no greater joy than to hear that my children walk in truth . . . We therefore ought to receive such, that we might be fellow helpers to the truth."

God wants us to be in good health. He also wants our souls to prosper. God wants us to get into a relationship with Him. He wants us to move closer and closer towards Him. Our purpose is to spread the word of God to others. God wants us to tell others about what the Bible says about Him. Let's not only talk about the word; let's be doers of God's word.

DAY 17:
(January 16)

Matthew 1: 18-21

"Now the birth of Jesus Christ . . . When His mother Mary was espoused to Joseph, before they came together, she was found with child of the Holy Ghost. But while he thought on these things, behold, the angel of the Lord appeared unto him in a dream, saying . . . fear not . . . for that which is conceived in her is of the Holy Ghost. *And she shall bring forth a Son, and . . . call His name JESUS: for He shall save His people from their sins."*

I would like to take the time to say, "Happy Dr. Martin Luther King Jr. Day!" This is a very important day of our African American heritage. Today, we must reflect and meditate on all the struggles and dreams Dr. King shared in making this a better world to live in. We must continue the vision for equality towards all people. I pray that the Lord will hear our prayer for a peaceful United States of America.

This scripture is especially for those who may not know the complete story of Jesus' birth. We are excited to learn more about the Bible and their Lord and Savior, Jesus Christ.

DAY 18:
(January 17)

John 3: 16-21

"*For God so loved the world that He gave His only begotten Son, that whosoever believes in Him should not perish, but have everlasting life.* For God sent not His Son into the world to condemn the world; but that the world through Him might be saved. For every one that does evil hates the Light . . . But he that does truth comes to the Light . . . that they are made in God."

God loves the world and all of His creations. He loves us so much; He gave His only begotten Son so that we might be saved. He wants us to do the things that are right and pleasing unto Him. He does not want us to go to hell. We were created for His purpose. Let's try to remember this scripture and tell it to all people we meet throughout our lives.

DAY 19:
(January 18)

*Joshua 1: 7-9

"Only be thou strong . . . to do according to all the law . . . that you may prosper wherever you go. *This book of the law shall not depart out of your mouth; but you shall meditate in it day and night, that you may observe to do according to all that is written in it*. . . for the Lord God is with you wherever you go."

Meditate on the word of God (The Bible) day and night. Learn as much about the Bible as you possibly can. Ask God to help you follow the Ten Commandments. We need to be doers of the word. Let's get serious about following God.

DAY 20:
(January 19)

Jeremiah 1: 4-9

"Before I formed you in the belly I knew you; and before you came forth out of the womb I sanctified you, and ordained you a prophet to the nations . . . for you shall go wherever I send you, and do whatever I command you shall speak. Be not afraid of their faces: for I am with you to deliver you, says the Lord . . . I have put My words in your mouth."

God wants us to tell others about Him. (Tell others what He has done for you). He has ordained us from the time we were conceived in our mother's womb. We should not be afraid to speak His word because He is with us daily. Continue to study the Bible so we can talk to everyone about our Lord and Savior, Jesus Christ.

DAY 21:
(January 20)

Ecclesiastes 12: 1-14

"*Remember your Creator in the days of your youth, before the days of trouble come.* . . Then shall the dust return to the earth as it was: and the spirit shall return unto God who gave it . . . Fear God, and keep His commandments: for this is the whole duty of man. For God shall bring every work into judgment, with every secret thing, whether it is good, or whether it is evil."

Now is the time to get right with God. Our body was made from the dust of the ground; therefore, when we die our body will return to dust. God wants us to obey His commandments that we might return to Him. As we go through life, we do good and bad things. God will judge them all.

DAY 22:
(January 21)

*Psalms 122:1-9

"*I was glad when they said to me; Let us go into the house of the Lord.* Our feet shall stand within the gates . . . Pray for peace . . . Peace is with you. Because the house of the Lord, I will seek Your goodness."

On Sundays, let's get ready; to prepare our hearts, mind, body and soul, to be with the Lord. He deserves our best praise and worship. God is great and God is good. Let's go into His presence with thanksgiving.

DAY 23:
(January 22)

2 Corinthians 5:17-21

"*Therefore if any man be in Christ, he is a new creature: old things are passed away; behold all things are become new.* And all things are of God, who has reconciled the world to Himself by Jesus Christ, and has given to us the ministry of reconciliation . . . Now then we are ambassadors for Christ . . . that we might be made the righteousness of God in Him."

Once we accept God as our Lord and Savior, we become a new creation. God is the creator of everything and everybody. Therefore, He is still in control of everything and everybody. Today, all of our sins are passed away through the death of Jesus on the cross. This is our opportunity to make things right with God. God wants us to be His mouthpieces. He wants us to speak to the sinners and lead them to Christ. We are His ambassadors (speakers of His house).

DAY 24:
(January 23)

Proverbs 3:1-7

"My son, forget not my law; but let your heart keep my commandments: For length of days, and long life, and peace, shall they add to you . . . So you shall find favor and good understanding in the sight of God and man . . . *Trust in the Lord with all your heart; and lean not unto your own understanding. In all your ways acknowledge Him, and He shall direct your paths* . . . Be wise in your own eyes: fear the Lord, and depart from evil."

God wants us remember the Ten Commandments in our hearts. If God knows we are faithful to Him, we have the promise of peace and long life. We should let God direct our paths and lead our lives. When we did not know God, we tried doing things our way. Now, let's give Him a chance to show us the right way to live.

Prayer:

Heavenly Father, I want to thank You for this day that You have made. I will rejoice and be glad in it. Lord, You prepared me for this day, this life; and I thank You for it. Continue to lead and guide me into the pathways of righteousness. I love You Lord, I praise You, and I magnify You. I will continue to be your servant and go and do whatever You will have me to do. I say this prayer in the name of the Father, the Son, and the Holy Spirit, Amen, and Amen again.

DAY 25:
(January 24)

*_Philippians 4:9-13_

"Those things, which you have both learned, and heard, and seen in Me, do: and the God of peace shall be with you. But rejoice in the Lord. . . _I can do all things through Christ who strengthens me._"

God wants us to lean not to our own understanding, but to trust in Him for everything. Once we look back on our not-so-good situations, we will see how the Lord stepped in to help us. God is our strength and our salvation.

DAY 26:
(January 25)

Matthew 6: 24-34

"Therefore I say unto you, Take no thought for your life, what you shall eat, or what you shall drink, or what you shall put on . . .the fowl of the air: they sow not . . . yet your heavenly Father feeds them. Are you not better than them? Consider the lilies of the field; how they grow . . . Therefore, if God clothes the grass of the field. . .He will clothe you. Therefore take no thought, saying, what shall we eat? Or, what shall we drink? Or how shall we be clothed?"

Your heavenly Father knows that we have need of all these things. *But seek ye first the kingdom of God, and his righteousness; and all these things shall be added unto you.* Take therefore no thought for the tomorrow; for the tomorrow will take care of itself.

I personally believe this passage of scripture speaks volumes. God is telling us to concentrate on Him. He will supply all of our needs, according to His riches in glory. If He takes care of the plants and animals; why can't we believe He will take of us? God loves us so much, that He gave His only begotten Son. He wants us to trust Him in every aspect of our lives. We should love God with all our hearts, minds, bodies and souls.

DAY 27:
(January 26)

Proverbs 18: 20-24

"A man's belly shall be satisfied with the fruit of his mouth; and with the increase of his lips shall he be filled. *Death and life are in the power of the tongue: and they that love it shall eat the fruit thereof.* Whoever finds a wife finds a good thing, and obtains favor with the Lord . . . A man that has friends must show himself friendly: and there is a friend that sticks closer than a brother."

We must speak life into our own lives and into our own situations. Our tongues have the power to bring forth life or bring down death. God wants us to clearly understand the power we have over life's situations. When we do the right thing by others; such as our spouse or friends; then we will find favor with the Lord.

***1 Corinthians 10: 21-26**

"You cannot drink of the cup of the Lord, and the cup of the devil: you cannot be partakers of the Lord's table, and the table of devils. Do we provoke the Lord to jealousy? Let no man seek his own, but every man another's wealth . . . *For the earth is the Lord's, and the fullness thereof.*"

God wants us the serve Him and Him alone. If we do things that are evil, then God will have nothing to do with us. We, as God's children, should love one another and look out for each other's well-being. Everything and everybody belongs to the Lord.

DAY 29:
(January 28)

Mark 8: 34-38

"Whosoever will come after me, let him deny himself, and take up his cross, and follow Me. For whosoever will save his life shall lose it; but whosoever shall lose his life for My sake and the gospel's, the same shall save it. *For what shall it profit a man, if he gain the whole world, and lose his own soul?* Whoever is ashamed of Me and My words. . .Then the Son of man will be ashamed of him"

TRUST in the Lord with your whole heart. Don't worry or be concerned with daily, basic everyday things. God is ordering our footsteps and our lives. He has commanded us to put our lives into His hands. If we deny God; on earth, then when we die, He may deny us. Let's pray to God for the will to "let go and let God" have His way with us.

DAY 30:
(January 29)

Psalm 121

"*I will lift up my eyes to the hills, from where my help come; my help comes from the Lord, which made heaven and earth.* He will not suffer your foot to be moved . . . The Lord is our keeper: The Lord is our shade . . . The Lord shall preserve us from evil: He will preserve our soul. The Lord will preserve our going out and our coming in, from this time forth, and even for evermore."

All we have to do is depend on God for everything. He will provide all of our needs. He will keep us emotionally, financially, physically, psychologically, and mentally. We serve a great big God who can do all things. He loves us very much.

DAY 31:
(January 30)

Hebrews 11:1-6

"*Now faith is the substance of things hoped for, the evidence of things not seen* . . . Through faith we understand the worlds were framed by the word of God, so that things which are seen were not made of things which do appear . . . But without faith it is impossible to please Him: for he that comes to God must believe that He is, and that He rewards them that diligently seek Him."

We must believe in God wholeheartedly. When we pray, we must believe that God hears us and that He will answer that prayer. If we do not have that faith, then it is impossible to please God. God made the world and everything in it. Let's believe God for everything.

DAY 32:
(January 31)

*Exodus 3:14-15

"And God said to Moses, *I AM that I AM*: And God said to Moses, The Lord of your father, the God of Abraham, the God of Isaac, and the God of Jacob: this is my name for ever and this is my memorial unto all generations."

God has established His name as: "I AM." He sent Moses to let the people know who He should be referred as. He set His name as "I AM", throughout all generations. Whatever your situation, God *is* that for you. If you are sick, I AM is your healer. If you need counsel, I AM is your lawyer. If you need finances, I AM is your provider. And the list goes on and on and on. Trust Him, because He is "THE GREAT I AM".

Today, I had planned on ending my morning inspirations. I personally believed everyone had had enough and was satisfied with continually studying the word of God on their own. As I proceeded to confirm this idea, my intuition was wrong. It was just the opposite. My children and best friends have asked if I would continue to send them the morning messages. I thank God for allowing me to be an inspiration to someone, in His name. I thank God for using me for His glory. I am so proud to say, "I love God and I know He loves me."

Prayer:

Lord, help me to do Your will. Continue to give me the messages to send out to Your people. Don't let me say or write anything that is not from You. I pray right now that I will be able to continue this process for the rest of the year. JESUS! Hallelujah! GLORY! Thank you Jesus! Thank you for this divine assignment. This has confirmed to me that You are in control of this book. I thank you God for Your mercy in my life. I say this prayer in Jesus' name; Amen, and Amen again.

DAY 33:
(February 1)

1 Thessalonians 5:14-18

"Support the weak, be patient towards all men. See that none render evil for evil to any man; but ever follow that which is good, both among you, and to all men . . . Pray without ceasing. In everything give thanks: for this is the will of God in Christ Jesus concerning you."

God wants us to treat everyone equally. He is watching how we treat one another. Keep praying to God to help you with your attitude. Whatever is in our hearts, take it to the Lord in prayer. He is concerned about each and every one of us.

DAY 34:
(February 2)

*2 Corinthians 4:14-18

"Knowing that He which raised up the Lord Jesus shall raise up us also by Jesus, and shall present us with You. For all things are for your sake . . . but though our outward man perish, yet the inward man is renewed day by day . . . while we look not at the things which are seen, but at the things which are not seen: For the things which are seen are temporal; but the things which are not seen are eternal."

God is saying that He rose up His Son Jesus from the cross. In that manner, He will raise us up also. We have to have faith through all of our everyday situations. What we see is temporary; but the things we can't see are forever. As our physical body is dying and will perish, the inward man; the soul, will live on after death.

DAY 35
(February 3)

*Acts 2:16-21

"This is what was spoken by the prophet Joel; and it shall come to pass in the last days, says the God, "I will pour out of My spirit upon all flesh: and your sons and daughters shall prophesy, and your young men shall see visions, and your old men shall dream dreams: And I will show wonders in the heaven above, and signs in the earth beneath . . . And it shall come to pass, that whoever call on the name of the Lord shall be saved."

We are saved by an awesome and mighty God. He is able to perform signs, wonders, and miracles, just as He did in the days of old. He promises that He will pour out His spirit upon us. He will show us the same signs He showed the people in the Bible. Let's call on His name *now*, and take Him at His word to save us.

DAY 36:
(February 4)

Proverbs 16:2-7

"All the ways of a man are clean in his own eyes; but the Lord weighs the spirits. Commit your works to the Lord, and your thoughts will be established. The Lord has made all things. . .Every one that is proud in heart is an abomination to the Lord . . . and by the fear of the Lord men depart from evil. When a man's ways please the Lord, He makes even his enemies to be at peace with him."

The Lord looks at the heart of man. We cannot see the things that God is concerned about, in us. He wants us to depart from our evil ways. When we show God we are sincere; He will be pleased with us. Let's examine ourselves and be for-real with God.

DAY 37:
(February 5)

James 4:10-17

"Humble yourself in the sight of the Lord . . . and He shall lift you up. Speak no evil to one another. . . There is one lawgiver, who is able to save and to destroy. . . Therefore to him that knows to do well, and does not, to him it is sin."

God has His eyes in every place. He sees our hearts. We must earnestly humble ourselves unto the Lord. He wants to live with us forever. Let's not be judges of one another. God is the only judge of people. Do not boast about yourself. We should live our lives loving, praising, and worshipping God.

DAY 38:
(February 6)

Hosea 4:1-6

"*My people are destroyed for lack of knowledge: because thou hast rejected knowledge*. I will also reject them. . .seeing that you have forgotten the law of God, I will also forget your children."

We are supposed to be children of God, but do not truly seek after Him. God wants us to diligently seek His face. God says if we do not return to His way, then He will forget about us and our children.

DAY 39:
(February 7)

Ecclesiastes 9:10-18

"Whatever your hands find to do; do it. . . for there is no work, nor device, nor knowledge, nor wisdom, in the grave. For man also knows not his time: as the fishes that are taken in an evil net, and as the birds that are caught in the snared in an evil time . . . Wisdom is better than strength: nevertheless the poor man's wisdom is despised, and his words are not heard . . . Wisdom is better than weapons of war."

We are all born for God's purpose. He has given each and every one of us a specific gift. Whatever we are good at, God expects us to do it with our whole heart. Do whatever is assigned to you. God is watching us and wants to give us the wisdom to do what is right and pleasing to Him.

DAY 40:
(February 8)

*Ephesians 4:4-8

"There is one body, and one Spirit, even as you are called in one hope of your calling; One Lord, one faith, one baptism, One God and Father of all, who is above all, and through all, and in you all. He says, "*When He ascended up on high, He led captivity captive, and gave gifts unto men.*"

There is but one God. He is the Lord of us all. He is the one who saves us and gives us our spiritual gifts. When Jesus died and was resurrected, He freed us from our sins and gave us all specific gifts. Pray and ask God to show you what it is He wants you to do for His kingdom.

DAY 41:
(February 9)

Psalm 14

"The fool has said in his heart, *there is no God.* They are corrupt . . . The Lord looked down from heaven upon the children of men, to see if there were any that did understand, and seek God. They are all gone aside . . . there is none that does good, no, not one."

God wants us to learn as much about Him as we possibly can. He will return and look to see who actually has *true* faith. Many people claim to know God, but their actions and behaviors say something different. Do as the Bible instructs you to do. It will be pleasing to God.

DAY 42:
(February 10)

*Numbers 23:19

"God is not a Man, that He should tell a lie; neither the Son of Man that He should repent: have He said, and not done it? Or have He spoken, and not make it good?"

God tells us many things in His word (The Bible). He wants us to believe what is written. He loves us and will be our help in the time of need. God will provide whatever we need. Let's trust God at His word and pray for the faith to believe.

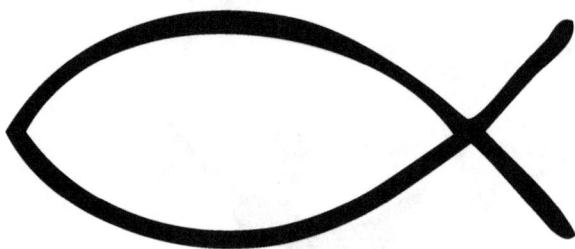

DAY 43:
(February 11)

Philippians 2:5-8

"Let this mind be in you, which was also in Christ Jesus . . .Who, being in the form of God, thought it not robbery to be equal with God . . . But made Himself of no reputation, and took on the form of a servant, and was made in the likeness of men . . . He humbled himself, and became obedient, unto death, even the death of the cross."

God wants to let us know that He made us in His image and likeness. He came down to earth, in the form of a man. He went through everything we are going through today. He was obedient, and He expects us to do the same. The idea is for us to love God with all our hearts, minds, bodies and souls.

DAY 44:
(February 12)

1 John 1:5-10

"This then is the message which we have heard of Him, and declare into you, that God is light, and in Him is no darkness at all . . . If we say that we have fellowship with Him, and walk in darkness, we lie, and do not the truth: *But if we walk in the light, as He is in the light, we have fellowship one with another, and the blood of Jesus Christ His Son cleanse us from all sin . . . If we confess our sins, He is faithful and just to forgive us our sins, and to cleanse us from all unrighteousness.* If we say that we have not sinned, we make Him a liar, and His word is not in us."

God is the Love. God is also (the) Light. God is the Light of this world and the Light that is in us all. We cannot walk in darkness (sin) and claim to be in and of God. Jesus Christ dies on the cross to cleanse us of our sins, therefore allowing us to walk in the Light of the Lord. All of us have sinned and must come to the Father and ask for forgiveness. Let's be truthful with ourselves and repent to God and ask for His Light.

DAY 45:
(February 13)

1 Corinthians 2:9-12

"But as it is written, *Eyes hath not seen, nor ears heard, neither have entered into the hearts of man, the things which God hath prepared for them that love Him* . . . Now we have received, not the spirit of the world, but the spirit which is of God; that we might know the things that are freely given to us of God."

We were made in the image of God. God is a spirit; therefore, we are made of the spirit. Our human minds cannot comprehend the wonderful things God has in store for us who love Him and follow after Him. We can get what God has for us, once we acknowledge Him as our Lord and King.

I would like to take the time to thank my Lord and Savior Jesus Christ. I usually pray all the time, but today I feel the urge to say the same prayer Jesus taught the disciples:

Prayer:

Our Father, which art in heaven, Hallowed be thy name . . .

DAY 46:
(February 14)

*St. Luke 6:35-38

"Love your enemies, and do good, and lend, hoping for nothing again; and your reward will be great . . . Be merciful, as your Father also is merciful. Judge not, and you shall not be judged: condemn not, and you shall not be condemned: forgive, and you shall be forgiven. *Give, and it shall be given unto you; good measures, pressed down, and shaken together, and running over, shall men give into your bosom.*"

God is merciful and just. He wants us to do unto others, as we would have them do unto us. Do the right thing to the best of your ability. Treat others as you would want to be treated. God watches over us and sees everything we do. Remember, man looks at the outward things, but God looks at the heart.

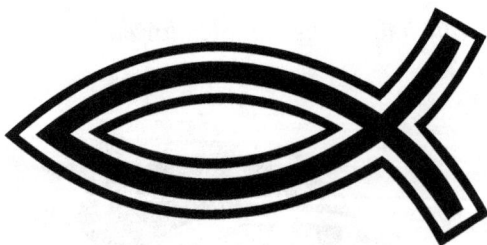

DAY 47:
(February 15)

James 1:17-22

"*Every good gift and every perfect gift is from above, and comes down from the Father of lights...* let every man be swift to hear, slow to speak, slow to wrath: For the wrath of man works not the righteousness of God. But are doers of the word and not hearers only, deceiving your own selves."

Everything comes from God. He is the giver of all gifts. When we receive a spiritual gift from God, we should be grateful and thank God wholeheartedly. Many people claim to be followers of God, but do not show it in their everyday lives. God wants us to live the way His word is instructing us to.

DAY 48:
(February 16)

Hebrews 13:1-8

"Let brotherly love continue. Remember them that are in bonds. . . and them which suffer adversity. . .Let your conversation be without covetousness. . .for He has said, *I will never leave you, nor forsake you . . . Jesus Christ the same yesterday, today, and forever.*"

We are all the same in the eyes of God. He sees us as brothers and sisters in Him. He promises us that He will never leave us nor forsake us. We can depend on God for everything. He will be there when everyone else lets us down. Love family, friends, and strangers as you would love God.

DAY 49:
(February 17)

*Matthew 18:18-22

"Verily I say unto you, whatever you bind on earth shall be bound in heaven: and whatever you shall loose on earth shall be loosed in heaven. Again I say to you, that if two of you agree on earth as touching any thing that they shall ask, it shall be done for them of my Father which is in heaven. *For where two or three are gathered together in My name, there am I in the midst of* them."

God wants us to be our brother's keeper. Don't look at the faults of others, but be concerned about each other. We should all learn to pray for one another. God promises us that if we touch and agree in faith, He will be in the midst. We should come together and pray and watch out for each other.

DAY 50:
(February 18)

Mark 13:30-33

"Verily I say unto you, that this generation will not pass, till all these things have been done. *Heaven and earth shall pass away: but My word shall not pass away.* But the day and that hour knows no man, no, not the angels which are in heaven, neither the Son, but the Father. Take heed, watch and pray: for you do not know when the time is."

The Lord is soon to return. There are many signs that we are living in the end of time. God says, everything on this earth will fade away, but His word will continue on, for other generations. As the coming of the Lord draws near, we are instructed to continue to watch and pray. God loves us enough to prepare us for His coming.

DAY 51:
(February 19)

Proverbs 18:7-10

"A fool's mouth is his destruction, and his lips are the snare of his soul. The words of the talebearer are as wounds and they go down into the innermost parts of the belly . . . *The name of the Lord is a strong tower: the righteous runs into it, and is safe.*"

The tongue is as wicked as a two-edged sword. The words we say about each other will either harm or bless one another. When we say things that hurt each other, it affects us down to the soul. God says if we would come to Him in our times of hurt, harm, or danger, He would protect us. That is a blessing from the Lord. Let's pray one for another, that we may only say things that are good towards each other.

Prayer:

Father, in the name of Jesus, we come to You today to give You praise, glory, and honor for watching over us while we slept last night. We thank You Lord for waking us up this morning, still in our right mind. Father, You said, in all things give thanks unto You. We're coming to You this morning with an honest, open heart. We love You, God. Help us to be a better person, a child of God after Your own heart. We want to be Your servant. We want to serve You, Lord, with our whole heart, from the bottom of our heart. We want to be more like You. Help us Lord to say, and do what You would have us to do, and we pray for increased faith. We pray for healing in our body. God give us more time to serve You and lift Your name up high. Father, in the name of Jesus, we thank You for this prayer and all things. In Jesus' name we pray. Amen, and Amen again.

DAY 52:
(February 20)

*Roman 13:1-4

"Let every soul be subject to the higher powers. For there is no power but of God: the powers that be are ordained of God. Whoever resists the power resists the ordinance of God: and they that resists shall receive damnation . . ."

We are subject to a higher power, which is God. He is the ruler of our souls. We should not resist this power, and we should become subject to Him. When we reject Him, He will reject us.

DAY 53:
(February 21)

John 8:30-32

"As He spoke these words, many believed in Him. Then Jesus to those who believed on Him said, "*If you continue in My word, then are you My disciples indeed; And you will know the truth, and the truth will make you free.*"

Believe in God with all your heart, mind, and soul. He tells us to believe in Him, and we will know the truth. We will know how to live right. Once we follow His commandments, we will be free.

DAY 54:
(February 22)

Revelation 1:1-3

"The Revelation of Jesus Christ, which God gave to him, to show to His servants things which must shortly come to pass; and He sent and signified it by His angel to His servant John: Who bare record of the word of God, and of the testimony of Jesus Christ, and of all things that he saw. *Blessed is he that reads, and they that hear the words of this prophecy, and keep those things which are written within: for the time is at hand.*"

We are living in the last days. There are many signs right before our eyes that tell us this. God wants us to read the Bible and keep His commandments until He returns. Let's pray for the will to study God's word and do what it says. He wants all of us to have eternal life.

DAY 55:
(February 23)

*Matthew 6:25-33

"Therefore I say to you, take no thought for your life, what you will eat; neither for the body, what you will put on. The life is more than meat, and the body more than raiment . . . For all these things do the nations of the world seek after: and your father knows that you have need of these things. *But seek the kingdom of God; and all these things will be added to you . . . For where your treasure is, there will your heart be also.*"

God will take care of all of our needs. We pay too much attention to the things of this world. These things will fade away, but the things of God will last into eternity. If God will provide for the birds, plants, and animals, He will surely care for us. We are made in His image; therefore, He will care for us and supply all of our needs.

DAY 56:
(February 24)

2 Corinthians 5:1-10

"We know that if our earthly house of this tabernacle were dissolved, we have a building of God; a house not made with hands, but eternal in the heavens. Therefore we are always confident, knowing that while we are at home in the body, we are absent from the Lord. *For we walk by faith, not by sight . . . I would rather be absent from the body, and to be present with the Lord.* For we must all appear before the judgment seat of Christ; that every one may receive the things done in his body, according to what he has done, whether it be good or bad."

We must pray and ask God to give us a heart to trust Him. Let's pray for an increase in faith. We will all be judged for everything we do, in this tabernacle. Our tabernacle is our body. So, let's pay attention to all that we do while living on earth. Remember, being absent in the body; is being present with God.

DAY 57:
(February 25)

Jeremiah 29:11-13

"For I know the thoughts that I think toward you, says the Lord, thoughts of peace, and not of evil, to give you an expected end . . . And you shall seek me, and find me, when you search for me with all your heart."

God loves us. He wants to let us know that it is safe to seek after Him, with our whole heart. He will give us His best; therefore, we should do the same. Let's totally trust in the Lord.

Yesterday; Friday, February 24, I received the blessing from the Lord, which I have been searching for, for the past three to four years. My pastor has decided to ordain me. He told me he would have an ordination ceremony; which gave me enough notice to invite my family and loved ones. The feelings that came upon me were very sacred and divine. I felt like crying and shouting at the same time. I have been waiting patiently for God to officially call me to ministry. I would like to thank God for allowing me this opportunity to serve Him with all of my heart, mind, body, and soul. I promise to do, say, and act only as He would have me to do. I want to decrease and allow God to increase in everything surrounding His ministry. Whatever I am called to do, I will do it with the love of God first and to be true and genuine at all times. Thank you, Jesus, for hearing my heart. I will serve you with an open heart. God bless those who are reading these inspirational messages. I love my wife. I thank her for being a part of my spiritual journey, at this special moment of my life. Let's go out and win souls for Christ and be the best that God has called us to be.

DAY 58:
(February 26)

Galatians 6:1-9

"Brothers and sisters, if a man be overtaken in a fault, those who are spiritual, restore them in a spirit of meekness; considering yourself, lest you will also be tempted. Bear one another's burdens, and so fulfill the law of Christ . . . Be not deceived; *God is not mocked: for whatever a man sows, that will he also reap . . . And let us not be weary in well doing: for in due season we will reap, if we faint not.*"

Many people think they know everything there is to know about God, but that is far from the truth. We need to all humble ourselves and pray for forgiveness. God is looking for His people to humble themselves unto Him. He wants us to help each other out in every way we can. We will make it, if we don't give up.

*_Matthew 7:7-11_

"Ask, and it will be given you; seek, and you will find; knock, and it will be opened to you: For every one that asks, receives; and he that seeks finds . . . If you, being evil know how to give good gifts to your children, how much more will your Father, which is in heaven give good things to them that ask Him?"

God is awesome, mighty and powerful. He is available to supply all _of our needs. Trust Him. We should develop such a relationship with God to be able to ask for whatever our need is. He loves us with unconditional love. We should love Him with all of our hearts, minds, and souls._

DAY 60:
(February 28)

James 5:13-16

"Is any among you afflicted? Let him pray. Is any merry? Let him sing psalms. Is any sick among you? Let him call the elders of the church; and let them pray over him, anointing him with oil in the name of the Lord . . . Confess your faults to one another, that you may be healed. *The effectual fervent prayer of a righteous man avails much.*"

God wants us to pray for everything. If we are sick, pray for healing. We need to pray for one another. If we pray with an open heart, God will hear us and help us. He instructs us to take the sick to the elders of the church for prayer. Let's repent and start fresh with God today.

DAY 61:
(February 29)

Romans 14:8-13

"For whether we live, we live unto the Lord; and whether we die, we die unto the Lord: whether we live therefore, or die, we are the Lord's. For this end Christ both died, and rose . . . For it is written, *as I live, says the Lord, every knee shall bow to Me, and every tongue shall confess to God.*"

Jesus died for us. He died for our sins. On the third day He rose so that we might receive eternal life. Therefore, we belong to God to live according to His will for us. One day, we all will have to bow down and worship Him. Today is the day to start loving God as He loves us.

DAY 62:
(March 1)

*Proverbs 8:17-23

"*I love them that love Me; and those that seek Me early shall find Me* . . . My fruit is better than gold, yes, than fine gold; and My revenue than choice silver. I lead the way of righteousness . . . I was set up from everlasting, from the beginning."

God is the beginning and the end. He was here; on earth, before anything was ever made. His love is better than the finest gold. He is an everlasting God, ready to pour out His love on us. Those that seek Him will find Him.

DAY 63:
(March 2)

*Luke 18:16-27

"But Jesus called them, and said, suffer little children to come to Me, and forbid them not: for such is the kingdom of God. Verily I say unto you, whoever will not receive the kingdom of God as a little child will not enter in . . . they that have riches shall enter into the kingdom of God. *For it is easier for a camel to go through a needle's eye, than for a rich man to enter into the kingdom of God . . . And He said, The things which are impossible with men are possible with God."*

We look at things from a humanistic view; whereas, God sees things in the spirit. He wants us to depend on Him for everything. Just like little children depend on their parents to care for them, so does our Father God want us to depend on Him? God wants us to have total faith in Him.

DAY 64:
(March 3)

2 Corinthians 13:4-6

"Though He was crucified through weakness, yet He lives by the power of God. We also are weak in Him, but we shall live with Him by the power of God. *Examine yourselves, whether you are in faith: prove your own selves. Know your own selves, how that Jesus Christ is in you, except you become reprobates."*

The power of God raised Jesus from the dead. He is the strength of our salvation. We need to examine ourselves to see what we really believe about God. If we don't develop our own personal relationship with Him, we are just living by someone else's standards. We are the children of a mighty God.

DAY 65:
(March 4)

Isaiah 55:6-11

"Seek the Lord while He may be found, call upon Him while He is near: Let the wicked forsake his way, and the unrighteous man his thoughts . . . *For My thoughts are not your thoughts, neither are your ways My ways, says the Lord, . . . So shall My words be that goes forth out of My mouth: it shall not return unto Me void, but it shall accomplish that which I please, and it shall prosper in the thing whereto I send it."*

Today is the day to commit to God. He is near to us every day. We think in the natural; whereas, God is spirit. His thoughts are not like our thoughts, and His ways are not like our ways. His word (The Bible), is spirit and the truth. Whatever is written within the Bible tells us everything we need to know to be in the spirit with the Lord. Let's trust in His word and keep our minds on things in the spirit.

DAY 66:
(March 5)

Colossians 3:1-5

"If you are raised with Christ; seek those things which are above, where Christ sits on the right hand of God. *Set your affection on things above, not on things on the earth.* For you are dead, and your life is hid with Christ in God. When Christ who is our life, shall appear, then shall we also appear with Him in glory."

When we are born again, we live with God. Once we become a child of God; we become one with Him. He lives in us, as we live in Him. Jesus sits at the right-hand of God. Therefore; while living here on earth, we should clean-up our temple, so that we can have everlasting life with Christ Jesus, who is our God.

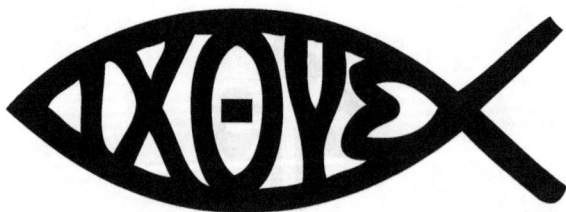

DAY 67:
(March 6)

*John 14:1-7

"Let not your heart be troubled: believe in God, believe also in Me. *In My Father's house are many mansions*: if it were not so, I would have told you. I go to prepare a place for you . . . I will come again, and receive you unto myself. . . Jesus said *I am the truth, and the life: no man comes to the Father, but by Me. If you know Me, you should have known My Father also.*"

God is three-in-one. He is God the Father, God the Son, and God the Holy Spirit. He explains when they saw Jesus, they saw the Father (God). He has returned unto God, to prepare a place for us. We will have eternal life with our Lord and Savior, Jesus Christ.

Prayer:

Lord, we come to You, this day, to give you thanks. We want to pray for our life and our family. God, You know all things. You said that You have eyes in every place. We are praying, Lord, for healing in our body. Touch everything that may prevent us from having a longer life here on earth. Touch the organs, arteries, veins, and blood in our body. Heal us Lord, from the crown of our head to the soles of our feet. Touch us Lord. And Lord, increase our faith in You. Increase our love for You and each other. Father, in the name of Jesus, touch and heal our family. Bless our family. Lord, pour out your spirit upon our children and loved ones. Save each and every one of them. Give them the desire to want to serve You. Increase their faith. God, we believe this prayer is already done, in Jesus' name. We will continue to give You all the glory, all the honor, and all the praise. Thank you, God, for allowing us to serve You. Continue to give us the desire to serve You, in the powerful, precious name of our Lord and Savior Jesus Christ, Amen.

DAY 68:
(March 7)

*Philippians 4:4-7

"Rejoice in the Lord always: and again I say Rejoice. Let your moderation be known unto all men, The Lord is at hand. *Be careful for nothing; but in everything by prayer and supplication with thanksgiving let your request be made known to God.* And the peace of God, which passes all understanding, shall keep your hearts and minds through Christ Jesus."

In all things, give thanks to the Lord. He is worthy to be praised. He tells us not to be anxious for anything. Don't be in a hurry for things to happen. He is in control of our destiny. Continue to pray for everything you want and need from the Lord. He will supply all of our needs. Trust in the Lord with your whole heart, mind, and soul.

DAY 69:
(March 8)

Genesis 17:1-7

"And when Abram was ninety years old and nine, the Lord appeared to Abram, and said unto him, I am the Almighty God; walk before Me, and be thou perfect. *And I will establish My covenant in their generations for an everlasting covenant, to be a God unto thee,* and thy seed after thee."

The Lord has promised us to be our God for generations through generations. We should tell our children about the Lord, and they should tell their children, and so-on and so-on. God has made this an everlasting covenant.

DAY 70:
(March 9)

Matthew 10:30-40

"But the very hairs of your head are all numbered. Whoever will confess Me before men, him will I confess also before My Father which is in heaven. But whoever deny Me before men, him will I also deny before my father which is in heaven . . . *He that finds his life shall lose it: and he that loses his life for My sake shall find it.* He that receives you receives Me, and he that receives Me receives Him that sent Me."

We are made in the image of God. He knows every hair that's on our heads. He is watching and listening to see if we are telling others about Him. If we deny Him, then He will deny us. When people reject us, they really are rejecting God. It is the God in us that people are receiving or denying.

DAY 71:
(March 10)

Hebrews 13:6-8

"So that we may boldly say, The Lord is my helper, and I will not fear what man will do to me. *Jesus Christ the same yesterday, and today, and forever.*"

No matter what trials we go through, we have the promise from God to help us. We do not depend on our own strength for any situation. We depend on God to fight our battles.

DAY 72:
(March 11)

1 Corinthians 15:51-58

"Behold, I show you a mystery; We shall not sleep, but we shall all be changed. In a moment, in the twinkling of an eye, at the last trump, for the trumpet shall sound, and the dead shall be raised incorruptible, and we shall be changed . . . Therefore . . . *be steadfast, unmovable, always abounding in the work of the Lord, . . . know that your work is not in vain.*"

God promises us that when He returns for us, we will be changed. The dead will rise first with Christ. Everyone who died in sin corruptible *will* rise. We will all become new again.

DAY 73:
(March 12)

James 2:21-26

"Was not Abraham our father justified by works, when he had offered Isaac his son upon the altar? And by works was faith made perfect . . . Abraham believed God . . . and he was called a friend of God . . . *For as the body without the spirit is dead, so faith without works is dead also.*"

Abraham trusted God to the point that he was willing to offer the death of his own son. God looked at this act of faith as special and called him His friend. God wants us to demonstrate how much we love Him through our works of faith.

DAY 74:
(March 13)

Isaiah 66:15-16

"For, behold, the Lord will come with fire, and with His chariots like a whirlwind to render His anger with fury, and His rebuke with flames of fire. For by fire and by His sword will the Lord plead with all flesh: and the slain of the Lord shall be many."

[He will come with flames of fire. The Lord wants us to be a part of His kingdom, but we must obey His commandments. Let's pray that we will not be consumed in His wrath of fire.]

Prayer:

Lord, the morning inspiration was hard to do yesterday. I promised myself; and especially You, that I would only write what You would have me to write. Well, I did just that. It felt hard, but I knew it came from You. I believe this message was necessary and right on time. Jesus, a few days ago, I added another friend. He actually called me to ask for clarification on the message. Lord, I have not spoken to him for over twenty years. It was amazing and a blessing to see how You moved through Your word. I believe everyone receiving the morning inspirations will receive a blessing from God. Lord, continue to use me for Your glory. Father, I am praying for my brother and friend, because he is going through some trying times. He needs You Lord and trusts You to lead and guide him through this transition. Help me God to continue to write only what You would have me to write. I pray that my children and everyone else receiving these messages will get a personal relationship with You, Lord. I pray this prayer and all prayers in the precious name of Jesus, Amen.

DAY 75:
(March 14)

*Revelation 1:7-8

"Behold, He comes with clouds; and every eye shall see Him, and they also which pierced Him: and all kindred of the earth shall wail because of Him . . . *I am Alpha and Omega, the Beginning and the ending . . . which is and which was, and which is to come, The Almighty.*"

The Lord is soon to return. His word says that when He returns, He will bring His wrath upon those who do not follow Him. Every person will see Him. He declares that He is all things to all people. Let's pray for an increase in our faith and for Him to adopt us into His kingdom.

DAY 76:
(March 15)

Romans 1:16-17

"For I am not ashamed of the gospel of Jesus Christ: for it is the power of God unto salvation to every one that believeth . . . as it is written, *the just shall live by faith.*"

The way to salvation is to know God and to serve Him . Through Christ Jesus, we are adopted into the kingdom of God. The word of God says that we should live our lives, simply believing in His word. Let's pray for increased faith.

ΩΑ

DAY 77:
(March 16)

Matthew 18:1-6

"At the same time came the disciples unto Jesus, saying, who is the greatest in the kingdom of heaven? And Jesus called a little child... *Verily I say unto you, except you be converted, and become as little children, you shall not enter into the kingdom of heaven. Whoever will humble himself as this little child, the same is greatest in the kingdom of heaven. And whoso shall receive one such little child in My name receives Me."*

Little children are a precious jewel from God. God wants us to turn our hearts and minds back to understand the humility of a child. They listen, obey, and are easy to teach. God wants us to be humble in all that we do.

DAY 78:
(March 17)

2 Timothy 2:11-15

"It is a faithful saying: For if we be dead with Him, we shall also live with Him: If we suffer, we shall also reign with Him: if we deny Him, he also will deny us . . . *Study to show yourself approved unto God, a workman that needed not be ashamed, rightly dividing the word of truth.*"

Jesus died on the cross for our sins. He was raised by the Father; therefore we were raised with him. If we deny Him, He will deny us. God wants us to study His word and get the understanding from Him. We will hear many preachers preach God's word, but we must read it and know it for ourselves. Let's pray for revelation knowledge of His word.

DAY 79:
(March 18)

Ephesians 2:1-9

"And you hath he quickened, who were dead in trespasses and sins; Wherein . . . you walked according to the prince of this world . . . but God who is rich in mercy . . . even when we were dead in sin . . . quickened us together with Christ." *For by grace you are saved through faith; and that not of yourselves: it is a gift of God."*

We all have done sinful things. God had mercy on us and adopted us into His kingdom of love. Even while we were sinners, God loved us enough to save us. It is a gift from God to be saved. Let's give praise with thanksgiving unto the Lord.

DAY 80:
(March 19)

Ephesians 4:29-32

"Let no corrupt communication proceed out of your mouth, but that which is good, that which is good to the use of edifying, that it may minister grace unto the hearers . . . Let all bitterness, and wrath, and anger, and clamor, and evil speaking. Be put away from you, with all malice. And be kind to one another . . . even as God for Christ's sake have forgiven you."

Pay attention to how you speak to others. Life and death is in the power of your tongue. God says to speak good things to one another and also to be kind. The Lord has done this to you; so, likewise, He wants us to do the same.

DAY 81:
(March 20)

John 1:1-5

"In the beginning was the Word, and the Word was with God, and the Word was God . . . All things were made by Him; and without Him was not anything made that was made. In Him was life; and life was the light of men."

The word was God and is God. The word is the light of God. God made everything and everybody. God is the beginning and the end; the first and the last, the Alpha and Omega. Let's pray for understanding of the word of God.

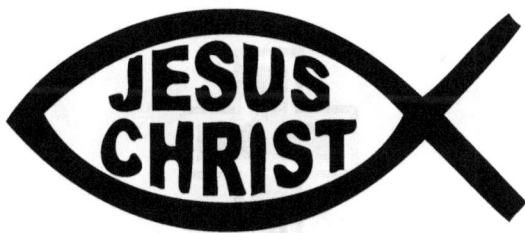

DAY 82:
(March 21)

Psalm 31

"In thee O Lord, do I put my trust; let me never be ashamed: deliver me . . . deliver me speedily . . . Pull me out of the net . . . Into your hand I commit my spirit . . . I will be glad and rejoice in thy mercy . . . Have mercy upon me . . . hide them in the secret of thy presence from the pride of man . . . *Be of good courage, and He shall strengthen your heart, all that hope in the Lord.*"

David, the writer of the Psalm, is telling a story of his life. He tells us how to deal with life's situations and to always trust in the Lord. He is having a personal conversation with God. Let's pray for a personal relationship with God for our lives.

DAY 83:
(March 22)

Deuteronomy 28:11-14

"And the Lord shall make thee plenteous in goods, in the fruit of thy body . . . The Lord shall open unto thee his good treasure . . . *And the Lord will make you the head, and not the tail; and you shall be above only, and you will not be beneath . . . And you shall not go aside from any of the words which I command you this day, to the right or to the left.*"

All God wants us to do is follow His word. If we obey the Ten Commandments, He will pour us out many blessings. He will put us on the top and make us the head of every situation. Let's pray for the will to follow God with honesty and love.

DAY 84:
(March 23)

*2 Corinthians 10:3-5

"For though we walk in the flesh, we do not war in the flesh: *(For the weapons of our warfare are not carnal, but mighty through God to the pulling down of strongholds)* Casting down imaginations and every high thing that exalts itself against the knowledge of God, and bringing into captivity every thought to the obedience of Christ."

All of the fights we are encountering in the flesh are from the spirit. God is fighting our battles daily. Our weapons are holy through Christ who strengthens us. Stay faithful to God, and He will give us the power to defeat our strongholds.

DAY 85:
(March 24)

*Proverbs 10:5-10

He that gathers in summer is a wise son . . . Blessings are upon the head of the just . . . The memory of the just is blessed . . . The wise in heart will receive commandments . . . *He that walks uprightly walks surely: but he that perverts his ways will be known."*

God is paying attention to everything we do. Nothing gets pass the eyes of the Lord. If we do not live right, it will be exposed. Let's pray for a serious relationship with our God.

DAY 86:
(March 25)

1 Samuel 12:20-25

"And Samuel said to the people, Fear not . . . And do not turn aside: for then you will go after vain things, which cannot profit nor deliver: for they are vain . . . *Only fear the Lord, and serve Him in truth with all your heart: for consider how great things He has done for you.*"

We should consider the way we walk through this life. Do not go after things that are vain, but the things pertaining to God. Serve the Lord with your whole heart, mind, and soul. God has kept us through all of our challenging days.

DAY 87:
(March 26)

1 Peter 3:8-15

"Finally, be of one mind, having compassion one of another, love as brothers, be pitiful, be courteous: Not rendering evil for evil . . . For the eyes of the Lord are over the righteous, and His ears are open unto their prayers . . . *But sanctify the Lord God in your heart: and be ready always to give an answer to every man that asks you an reason of the hope that is in you.*"

God wants us to love one another as He has loved us. He says to stay away from doing evil and He will bless us. But if we do evil, He will be against us. He will hear our prayers and pour us out blessings. Let's pray to know and understand His word to share with others who do not know about Him.

DAY 88:
(March 27)

1 Corinthians 13:11-13

"*When I was a child, I spoke as a child; I understood as a child, I thought as a child: but when I became a man, I put away childish things* . . . And now abide faith, hope, and charity, these three; but the greatest of these is love."

God wants us to think like men and put away childish behaviors. The attitude will help us move closer to the Lord. Once we recognize this concept, we will abide in faith, hope and charity. We must remember that God says, *love* is the greatest of them all.

DAY 89:
(March 28)

Proverbs 21:1-4

"The king's heart is in the hand of the Lord, as the rivers of water: he can turn it wherever He will. *Every way of a man is right in his own eyes: but the Lord ponders the hearts . . .* An high look, and a proud heart, and the plowing of the wicked, is sin."

God has all power. He can change the hearts and minds of the ones in charge. Man sees things in the flesh; whereas, the Lord sees the things in the spirit. God does not want us to act or feel better than anyone else. If we do, He considers it a sin. God wants us to be more like Him.

Luke 14:11-14

"*For whoever exalts himself shall be humbled; and he that humbles himself will be exalted . . .*" When you make a dinner or supper, call not your friends, nor your brother, neither your kinsmen, or your rich neighbors . . . But . . . call the poor, the maimed, the lame, the blind . . . for they cannot repay you."

God wants us to be humble in everything we do. If we humble ourselves, God will exalt us. He has instructed us to feed the poor; therefore, every chance we get, we shall do an act of kindness to someone in need.

DAY 91:
(March 30)

2 Thessalonians 3:1-5

"Finally, brethren, pray for us, that the word of the Lord may have free course, and be glorified, even as it is with you. And that we may be delivered from unreasonable and wicked men: for not all men have faith. But the Lord is faithful, who shall establish you, and keep you from evil . . . And the Lord direct your hearts into the love of God."

Let's pray for the Lord to have His way in our lives. He will *deliver* us from all evil. It is totally up to the Lord to do as He pleases with our lives. He, and He alone, is the source of our salvation.

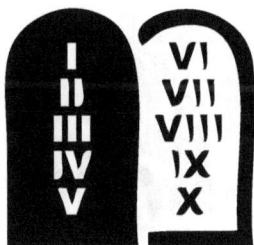

DAY 92:
(March 31)

*Ephesians 6: 1-4

"Children, obey your parents in the Lord, for it is right. *Honor your father and mother, which is the first commandment with promise.* That it may be well with you and you may live long on the earth. Fathers do not provoke your children to wrath, but bring them up in the training . . . of the Lord."

God has commanded us to honor our mothers and fathers. He will bless us with long life on the earth. Even as adults, we should follow this commandment. Fathers are commanded to teach their children the ways of the Lord and salvation.

DAY 93:
(April 1)

*Proverbs 9:9-11

"Give instruction to a wise man, and he will yet be wiser: teach a just man, and he will increase in learning. *The fear of the Lord is the beginning of wisdom: and the knowledge of the Holy Spirit understands* . . . and the years of thy life shall be increased.

Teach a wise man, and he will become wiser. Teach a just man, and he will increase his knowledge. To fear the Lord is the beginning of understanding who God is. That is the ultimate goal of the Lord—to have us seek after Him with our whole hearts, minds, and souls.

DAY 94:
(April 2)

Matthew 5:13-16

"*You are the salt of the earth*: but if the salt lost his savor, it is good for nothing, but to be cast out, and to be trodden under foot of men. *You are the light of the world . . . Let your light shine before men . . . and glorify your Father which is in heaven.*"

We are made in the image of God. He has made us His light here on earth. He wants us to let our light shine, so others may see Him. Pray that we continue to let the world see God in us and that we will make Him happy.

DAY 95:
(April 3)

John 8:12-16

"Then Jesus spoke . . . saying, *I am the light of the world: he that follows Me will not walk in darkness, but will have the light of life* . . . You judge after the flesh; I judge no man. And if I judge, My judgment is true: for I am not alone, but I and the Father that sent Me."

Jesus is the light that represents the good in the world. Satan is the darkness that represents the evil of the world. Jesus says He will not judge us; but when He does, it is from the Father. Let's pray to follow Jesus and to receive eternal life with our Father who art in heaven.

DAY 96:
(April 4)

2 Thessalonians 2:7-12

"*For the mystery of lawlessness is already at work* . . . then the lawless one will be revealed . . . The coming of the lawless one is according to the working of Satan, with all power and lying wonders . . . God will send them strong delusion, that they may believe the lie. *That they all may be condemned who did not believe the truth but had pleasure in unrighteousness.*"

We are living in the last days. The word of God says that God Himself will turn the minds of the unbeliever to accept the lies and deception of the devil, Satan. He wants us to believe the gospel of Jesus Christ and live it to the best of our ability.

Prayer:

Heavenly Father, I come to You with an open heart. I understand You want us to come to You in prayer with an open heart. I come to You for strength in continuing these morning inspirations. Please Lord, let me only send what You would have me to write. Many times, when the message is hard to write, I want to know if it from You or me. Lord, bless these messages and pour out Your spirit upon me to have the courage to write in the spirit. I will only give You the honor and the praise. Keep me and my family safe from the evil spirit that may try to come between us. I say this prayer in the precious name of Jesus, Amen.

DAY 97:
(April 5)

2 Timothy 2:7-12

"Consider what I say, and may the Lord give you understanding in all things . . . *This is a faithful saying: for if we died with Him, we shall also live with Him. If we endure, we shall also reign with Him, If we deny Him, He also will deny us.*"

If we learn the ways of God, He will give us His understanding. We must seek the kingdom of heaven for God's knowledge and wisdom. If we continue to follow His commandments, He will reign with us. We pray today never to deny the Lord, because we do not want Him to deny us.

DAY 98:
(April 6)

Mark 15:17-20

"And they clothed Him with purple; and they twisted a crown of thorns, put it on His head . . . And when they had mocked Him . . . they lead Him out to crucify Him."

Good Friday is considered the day Pilate turned Jesus over to the people; to be crucified. Once Jesus took His last breath, Satan lost what he thought was his power over man. Jesus took on our sin to make atonement with us. Good Friday is also considered Holy Week. We should be in constant prayer for a personal relationship with our Lord and Savior, Jesus Christ.

DAY 99:
(April 7)

Isaiah 26:2-4

"Open the gates that the righteous nation which keeps the truth may walk in. *You will keep him in perfect peace, whose mind is stayed on You. Trust in the Lord forever, for in the Lord JEHOVAH is everlasting strength.*"

The Lord wants us to keep our minds stayed on Him. He is the source of our strength. He promises to keep us in everlasting peace if we trust in Him. We can ask God to create in us a heart and mind to trust Him.

This message is delivered in the mighty name of Jesus. It is for everyone reading these morning inspirations":

Make plans to attend church on Sundays. Take all your concerns and worries to the Lord's house.

DAY 100:
(April 8)

Psalms 71:1-8

"In You O Lord, I put my trust; let me never be put to shame. Deliver me in Your righteousness . . . Be my strong refuge . . . Deliver me O God, out of the hand of the wicked . . . *Let my mouth be filled with Your praise and with Your glory all the day.*"

I will praise the Lord with my whole heart. I trust that the Lord will never make me ashamed of Him. I pray that God will keep me my family from hurt, harm, and danger. Hallelujah, Glory, to the King of Kings and the Lord of Lords, My God and my Father, Abba, Father.

DAY 101:
(April 9)

Luke 6:27-29

"But I say to you who hear: love your enemies, do good to those who hate you, *Bless those who curse you, and pray for those who spitefully use you.* To him who strike you on the one cheek, offer him the other also."

God wants us to be more like Him. He asks us to, "Do unto others, as we would have them do unto us." Let's pray for a heart and mind like our Father who art in heaven.

DAY 102:
(April 10)

Romans 14:1-4

"*Receive one who is weak in the faith, but not to disputes over doubtful things.* Who are you to judge another's servant? To his own master he stands and falls . . . For God is able to make him stand."

God does not want us to judge one another. We are all trying to understand how to live with, in, and for God. The things of God are spirit, which makes them hard to understand. God is the one who allows us to have the revelation knowledge to discern His ways. Let's pray for each other to receive God as He will allow us to.

DAY 103:
(April 11)

Romans12:1-2

"I beseech you therefore, brethren, by the mercies of God, that you *present your bodies a living sacrifice*, holy, acceptable to God, which is your reasonable service. And *do not be conformed to this world, but be transformed by the renewing of your mind, that you may prove what is that good and acceptable and perfect will of God.*"

God is holy and therefore expects us to become holy unto Him. We are required to present our lives to Him as holy, clean, and pure as possible. This means that we should not do the things like the sinners of the world. We should do godly things that will please our Father who art in heaven.

DAY 104:
(April 12)

Deuteronomy 8:1-11

"Every commandment which I command you today you must be careful to observe, that you may live and multiply . . . remember that the Lord your God led you all the way these forty years in the wilderness . . . So He humbled you . . . *When you have eaten and are full, then you should bless the Lord your God* . . . Beware, that you do not forget the Lord . . . which I command you today."

God continues to remind us to follow His commandments. He tested the Israelites while they were wandering in the wilderness to strengthen their faith. We should always give thanks to the Lord for everything we have. If it had not been for the Lord, we would have nothing. God could have allowed us to die in the wilderness, but He loves us. Thanks be to God for giving us life.

DAY 105:
(April 13)

*Proverbs 3:5-6

"Trust in the Lord with all your heart, and lean not on your own understanding; in all your ways acknowledge Him, and He shall direct your paths."

Trust the Lord with your whole heart. Do not try to figure God out. He is in total control of everything and everybody. Let God lead and guide your path today. He is the author and finisher of our faith.

DAY 106:
(April 14)

*Hebrews 4:9-13

"There remains therefore a rest for the people of God . . . Let us therefore be diligent to enter that rest . . . *For the word of God is living and powerful, and sharper than a two-edged sword, piercing even to the division of the soul and spirit . . . There is no creature hidden from His sight . . . all are naked and open to the eye of Him.*"

Jesus has gone into the heavens to prepare a place for us to rest in God. We are instructed to obey the commandments to enter this rest. The eyes of the Lord are in every place. Every one of us should look forward to eternal life with our Father God.

Prayer:

Our Father, Who art in heaven, hallowed be thy name, thy kingdom come, thy will be done, on earth, as it is in heaven. Give us this day, our daily bread. But, forgive us our trespasses, as we forgive those who trespass against us. And lead us not, into temptation, but deliver us from evil. For you are the kingdom, the power, and the glory, forever, and ever, Amen. (This is my favorite prayer.)

*1 Corinthians 11:1-3

"Imitate me, just as I imitate Christ. *But I want you to know that the head of every man is Christ, the head of woman is man, and the head of Christ is God."*

God is looking down from heaven at our actions. We are representing the order of God's creation our own way. Man has incorporated his own understanding into the scriptures to satisfy his own life. We should pray for understanding and obedience to God's word.

DAY 108:
(April 16)

Joshua 22:1-6

"Then Joshua called . . . the tribe of Manasseh, And he said to them, "You have kept all that Moses . . . commanded you . . . *But take careful heed to do the commandment and the law . . . to love your God, to walk in His ways . . . and to hold fast to Him with all your heart and with all your soul."*

Our soul belongs to the Lord. We are to love God with our *whole hearts, minds, and souls.* God is paying attention to those who diligently seek Him. We should seek the kingdom of God, and everything else in life will follow.

DAY 109:
(April 17)

Psalm 118:4-9

"Let those who fear the Lord now say, His mercy endures forever . . . The Lord is on my side; I will not fear. *It is better to trust in the Lord than to put confidence in man.* It is better to trust in the Lord."

The love of God is everlasting. All we have to do is believe in Him for everything. He promises to be with us through every situation. All we need to do is *trust him.*

DAY 110:
(April 18)

1 John 4:15-21

"Whoever confesses that Jesus is the Son of God, God abides in him, and he in God . . . God is love, and he who abides in love abides in God . . . there is no fear in love; but perfect love cast out fear . . . *If someone says, "I love God," and hates his brother, he is a liar; for he who does not love his brother whom he has seen, how can he love God whom he has not seen? He who loves God must love his brother."*

God is Love. Many of us say we love one person or another; therefore, should love God. *But,* if we do not love our fellow man, then how on earth can we profess to love the Lord? Let's pray for genuine love for our sisters and brothers.

DAY 111:
(April 19)

Matthew 25:35-45

"I was hungry and you gave me food; I was thirsty and you gave Me drink; I was a stranger and you took Me in I was naked and you clothed Me; I was sick and you visited Me; I was in prison and you came to Me. Then the righteous will answer Him saying, when did we see You hungry and thirsty? *And the King answered and said to them, Assuredly, I say to you, whenever you did it to one of My brothers, you did it to Me.*"

God is letting us know that when we serve His people, we may be entertaining His angels. Do unto others as you would have them do unto you. God has a watchful eye on everything we do for others. Let's treat each other with Godly love.

DAY 112:
(April 20)

Psalm 51:6-13

"Behold, You desire truth in the inward parts, and in the hidden part You will make me to know wisdom. Purge me with hyssop, and I shall be clean . . . Hide Your face from my sins . . . *Create in me a clean heart . . . and renew the right spirit in me.* Do not cast me away from Your presence . . . Then I will teach transgressors Your way."

The Lord is all knowing and all powerful. He knows our going in and coming out. He knows and sees everything we do. Our prayer today should be to ask God for a clean heart and a renewed spirit.

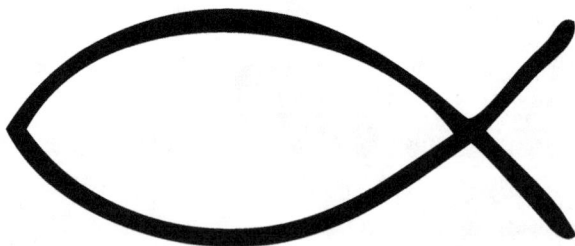

DAY 113:
(April 21)

Galatians 3:22-29

"But the Scriptures have confined all under sin that the promise by faith in Jesus Christ might be given to those who believe. But before faith came, we were kept under guard by the law . . . Therefore the law was our tutor to bring us to Christ . . . *For we are all sons of God through faith in Christ Jesus* . . . And if we are Christ's, then you are Abraham's seed."

Having faith in God is what keeps us in the kingdom of God. We receive faith through the power of God. The books of the Bible are the law(s) we should go by. Abraham believed in God's promises. If we have faith in God, we will receive the same blessing as Abraham because we are His seed.

DAY 114:
(April 22)

Ephesians 3:16-21

"That He would grant you, according to the riches of His glory . . . That Christ may dwell in your hearts through faith; that you, being rooted and grounded in love . . . to know the love of Christ . . . that you may be filled with all the fullness of God. *Now to Him who is able to do exceedingly abundantly above all that we ask or think, according to the power that works in us*, to Him be the glory."

God has all that we need to live in this world. We don't need to worry about things for daily living. Have faith in God, and He will supply all of our needs. Pray for the power of God to pour out His spirit upon us. We only need to have God to have life.

DAY 115:
(April 23)

John 10:7-12

"Jesus said to them . . . I am the door of the sheep . . . I am the door, if anyone enters by me shall be saved . . . *The thief does not come except to steal, and to kill, and to destroy. I have come that they may have life, and that they have it more abundantly.* I am the good shepherd . . ."

Jesus is the way, the truth, and the life. Anyone who wants eternal life must put their trust in His hands. The devil (the thief), has come to destroy the children of God. We must trust our Good Shepherd (The Lord), to protect us from the evil of this world.

DAY 116:
(April 24)

Philippians 2:10-15

"That at the name Jesus every knee should bow, of those in heaven, and those on the earth, and those under the earth, And every tongue should confess that Jesus Christ is Lord . . . *Do all things without complaining and disputing* . . . That you may become blameless and harmless children of God without fault in the midst of a perverse generation."

Every person and everything will bow down to the Lord. God wants us to be an example of righteousness. People of the world (non-Christians), murmur and complain about things of unimportance. God wants us to shine His Light upon all the earth as examples of His love.

Prayer:

Lord help us to shine Your Light upon this earth as an example of Your Love. We need Your help in giving us the will to follow Your commandments. God please forgive us of any sin we may have committed against You. Keep us and protect us from all evil. We love you. Amen.

James 1:22-27

"But be doers of the word, and not hearers only, deceiving yourselves . . . For he observes himself, goes away, and immediately forgets what kind of man he was . . . If anyone among you thinks he is religious, and does not bridle his tongue . . . this one's religion is useless. *Pure and undefiled religion before God and the Father is this: to visit orphans and widows in their trouble, and to keep oneself unspotted from the world."*

God is asking us to take a good look at ourselves. Do not hear His word and do nothing to tell others about it. We are required by God to spread His word. Don't talk bad about or down to anyone. God wants us to visit and minister to those who can't get out to hear His word.

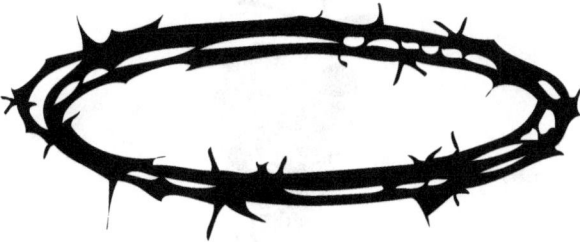

DAY 118:
(April 26)

*Proverbs 27:1-6

"*Do not boast about tomorrow, for you do not know what a day may bring forth.* Let another man praise you, and not your own mouth . . . Open rebuke is better than love carefully concealed. Faithful are the wounds of a friend, but the kisses of an enemy are deceitful."

We should not worry about tomorrow, because it is not promised to us. We should work towards establishing a relationship with God today. Be careful of people who appear to care about you. Sometimes, someone you think is your friend could be your enemy, and the one you think is an enemy can become a friend.

DAY 119:
(April 27)

Deuteronomy 31:6-8

"Be strong and of good courage, do not fear nor be afraid of them; for the Lord your God, He is the One who goes with you. He will not leave you nor forsake you . . . do not fear nor be dismayed."

The Lord is our strength in the time of need. We only need to know that we are His children. Wherever we go, He will be there to protect us. Keep God close to your heart, and He will never leave you.

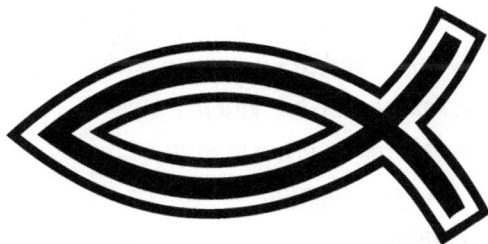

DAY 120:
(April 28)

*Ecclesiastes 3:1-8

"To everything there is a season, a time for every purpose under the heavens: A time to be born, and a time to die . . . A time to weep, and a time to laugh . . . A time to love, and a time to hate; a time of war, and peace."

There is a time and season for everything and everybody. We should look only to God for our existence. Whatever happens in this lifetime is all for the glory of the Lord. Let's pray for our hearts, minds, and souls to connect to God. He is the author and finisher of our lives.

Prayer:

Heavenly Father, I come to You this morning first to say thank You. God I want to continue to spread Your word to others. I need to have the boldness and courage to stand before people and speak Your word. Help me Lord, to gain confidence in myself. Give me more revelation knowledge of You. Assure me that I know what I need to know concerning You. I love You, Lord. I praise You Lord. God, You are my Father, and I will do Your will on earth and in heaven. Prepare my heart, mind, and soul to enter into the kingdom of heaven. I say this prayer in Jesus' name, Amen.

DAY 121:
(April 29)

*Joshua 24:13-18

"I have given you a land for which you did not labor . . . *Now therefore, fear the Lord, serve Him in sincerity and in truth . . . But as for me and my house, we will serve the Lord . . .* For the Lord our God is He who brought us . . . out of Egypt."

The Lord is good. He cares for us and wants us to serve Him and Him alone. The children of Israel wandered in the wilderness for forty years until God brought them out. He is the same God today, yesterday, and forever.

DAY 122:
(April 30)

Galatians 6:1-8

"If a man is overtaken in any trespass, you who are spiritual restore such a one in a spirit of gentleness, considering yourself lest you also be tempted. *Bear one another's burdens, and so fulfill the law of Christ* . . . he who sows to the Spirit will of the Spirit reap everlasting life."

God wants us to look out for one another. Whenever your fellow man is down in spirit, He wants us to lift him back up. In other words: we are our brother's keeper. Pray to God for a heart more like Him. He is watching everything we do.

DAY 123:
(May 1)

Psalm 118:24

"This is the day that the Lord has made; let us rejoice and be glad in it."

I have to admit that today while at the altar in the church this morning; it was hard to find a scripture to send out for the morning inspiration. I decided to send what the Lord was putting in my spirit at that particular time. I was amazed at the responses I received. I give all the honor and glory to my Lord and Savior, Jesus Christ. I will continue to send the messages as the Lord leads and guides my thoughts for His people. Amen.

DAY 124:
(May 2)

Philippians 1:3-11

"I thank my God upon remembrance of you, always in every prayer of mine making request for you all with joy . . . *Being confident of this very thing, that He who begun a good work in you will complete it until the day of Jesus Christ;* Being filled with the fruits of righteousness which are in Jesus Christ."

This scripture wants us to know that we are partakers of the blessing from Jesus Christ. In all of our situations, we should acknowledge the Lord. It will all be for the glory of God.

DAY 125:
(May 3)

*Romans 8:27-37

"He who searches our hearts knows what the mind of the Spirit is, because He makes intercession for the saints according to the will of God. *And we know that all things work together for the good of those who love God, to those who are called according to His purpose.* Yet in all these things we are more than conquerors through Him who loves us."

God knows all things that we go through in life. He knows about things before they even happen. Jesus Christ suffered and died on the cross; therefore we must also endure some things in life. God promises us that He has His eyes on us, and He will not let us go through more than we can handle. What we go through in life will only make us stronger physically, mentally, emotionally, and spiritually.

DAY 126:
(May 4)

*Ezekiel 18:25-32

"Yet you say, The way of the Lord is not fair . . . it is not My way which is not fair . . . I will judge you, O house of Israel . . ." *Repent and turn from all of your transgressions* . . . says the Lord God . . . For I have no pleasure in the death of one who dies . . . therefore turn and live."

The Lord lets us know it is not Him who condemns us; but we condemn ourselves. Everything we do is done through our own will. God gives us the opportunity to repent and get our lives back on track. He wants us to live with Him forever.

DAY 127:
(May 5)

1 Corinthians 15: 1-14

"Moreover, my brethren . . . I deliver to you first of all that which I received: that Christ died for our sins according to the Scriptures. *And that He was buried, and that He rose again the third day according to the Scriptures* . . . And if Christ is not raised, then our preaching is empty and your faith is also empty."

God wants us to believe in the Scriptures. Jesus died on the cross and was risen on third day. There are many stories in the Bible; and God wants us to tell them to others to help with their faith. Everything in the Bible is the word of God.

DAY 128:
(May 6)

*Luke 18:17-31

"*Assuredly, I say to you, whoever does not receive the kingdom of God as a little child will by no means enter it . . . For it is easier for a camel to go through the eye of a needle than for a rich man to enter the kingdom of God . . . But He said, The things which are impossible with men are possible with God . . .* all things that are written . . . will be accomplished."

God is letting us know that we must follow His commandments. We must present ourselves to God as little children. We must not seek to gain earthly wealth. All of our treasures must be heavenly. Let's pray for a heart and mind like Jesus.

DAY 129:
(May 7)

Hebrews 12:1-3

"*Therefore . . . let us lay aside every weight, and the sin which so easily ensnares us, and let us run with endurance the race that is set before us,* Looking unto Jesus, the author and finisher of our faith . . .*"*

We will endure difficult times in life. God wants us to lean on Him for strength to finish the task which is set before us. He endured the cross; therefore we must experience some trials. Look to the Lord who is the Author and finisher of our faith.

DAY 130:
(May 8)

2 John 1:1-11

"Because of the truth which abides in us and will be with us forever: *Grace, mercy, and peace will be with you . . . in truth and love. Whoever transgresses and does not abide in the doctrine of Christ does not have God.*

God is the truth and the life. Without God we are nothing. We must follow the commandments of the Lord and practice them with every effort of our being. Let's pray to God for strength and understanding of His doctrine.

Prayer:

God, give me the heart and mind to accept the things that I can't change and the knowledge to handle the things I can. Lord I just want to be able to deal with this life and be prepared for eternal life with You. There are many things coming against me as I try to follow Your will. I trust and believe that You will continue to fight my battles for me. I want to thank you for Your grace and mercy, Amen.

DAY 131:
(May 9)

*Proverbs 24:15-20

"Do not lie in wait, O wicked man . . . for a righteous man may fall seven times and rise again, but the wicked will fall by calamity. *Do not rejoice when your enemy falls, and do not let your heart be glad when he stumbles.* For there will be no reward for the evil man."

God is giving the wicked man a message to leave the righteous alone. The evil man will fall to his evil ways. A righteous man will continue to stand through the power of God. Let God handle your battles.

*1 Samuel 16:6-13

"So it was, when they came, that he looked at Eliab and said, "Surely the Lord's anointing is before him...." *For the Lord does not see as man sees; for man looks at the outward appearance, but the Lord looks at the heart* ... Then Samuel took the horn of oil an anointed him in the midst of his brothers ... and the Spirit of the Lord came upon David from that day forward."

God looks at the heart and soul of man. We look at the outward appearance. Never judge a person on his or her appearance. God may choose anyone He wants to be His vessel. Love the Lord and pray for His will to be done.

DAY 133:
(May 11)

Ephesians 4:28-32

"Let him who stole steal no longer, but rather let him labor
. . . Let no corrupt words proceed out of your mouth, but
what is good . . . And do not grieve the Holy Spirit of God
. . . *And be kind to one another, tenderhearted, forgiving one
another, even as God in Christ forgave you.*"

We were made in the image of God; therefore, we should try
to be more like Christ Jesus. We are to be careful how we
speak to people and treat each other as we would like to be
treated. God forgave us, so He wants us to do the same.

DAY 134:
(May 12)

Mark 7:14-23

"Hear Me and understand: *There is nothing that enters a man from outside which can defile him; but the things which come out of him, those are things that defile a man* . . . Because it does not enter his heart but his stomach . . . All these evil things come from within and defiles a man."

God wants us to be careful and watch what we say. We will receive many messages and ideas from others, but we shouldn't let them identify with our spirits. We are children of God; therefore, we should strive to be more like Him.

DAY 135:
(May 13)

May God bless you all!

1 Thessalonians 5:15-22

"*See that no one renders evil for evil to anyone, but always pursue what is good both for you and for all. Rejoice always, pray without ceasing, and in everything give thanks; for this is the will of God . . . Abstain from every form of evil.*"

God does not want us to fall into the traps of the devil. Satan has evil plans for our lives, but the Lord is our strength. He will be there to intercede on our behalf when evil is present. Trust in the Lord with constant prayer, and He will help. He knows the desires of our hearts.

Prayer:

Lord I come to You today, first to give You thanks. Lord, I don't want to send out morning inspirations from me. I want them to come from You. Help me Lord to move out of the way and allow You to have Your way in me to deliver Your word. Some mornings I have a hard time finding a message to share. When this happens I am afraid I am being in control of the messages. I want You God, to lead and guide me to the message You want the people to read. I will continue to trust in You only as I finish this 365-day of the Cooper's Morning Inspirational *book.*

*Romans 10:13-17

For whoever calls on the name of the Lord shall be saved. How then shall they call on Him in whom they have not believed? And how shall they believe in Him of whom they have never heard? And how shall they hear without a preacher . . . *So then faith comes by hearing, and hearing by the word of God."*

If you want to be saved; just call on the name of Jesus. He is waiting to accept you into His loving arms. It all depends on us to make the decision to follow His laws and be saved. We get the faith to believe God from going to church and listening to the preacher.

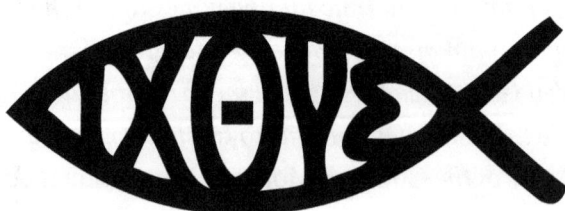

DAY 137:
(May 15)

*Nehemiah 8:8-10

"So they read distinctly from the book, in Nehemiah, who was the governor, Ezra the priest and the scribe, and the Levites who taught the people said to all the people, *"This day is holy to the Lord your God; do not mourn nor weep . . . for the joy of the Lord is your strength."*

Ezra was the priest who began to preach to the people. He formed a congregation and caused the people to understand the laws of Moses. God wants us to read the Bible, and He will give us the knowledge to understand what is written. Let's develop the will to search the scriptures for understanding that God is. He is waiting to give us revelation knowledge.

DAY 138:
(May 16)

Philippians 4:4-13

"Rejoice in the Lord . . . *Be anxious for nothing, but in everything by prayer and supplication, with thanksgiving, let your request be known . . . I can do all things through Christ who strengthens me.*"

The Lord is our strength and our help in time of need. We can always depend on the Lord to help us whenever we run into difficult situations.

DAY 139:
(May 17)

James 5:7-9

"Therefore be patient, brethren, until the coming of the Lord . . . *You also be patient, establish your hearts, for the coming of the Lord is at hand. Do not grumble against one another . . . the Judge is standing at the door."*

Again, the Lord is telling us to be patient. Be anxious for nothing. He wants us to get our lives in order, because Jesus is soon to return. Do not get into arguments with one another because God is the Judge of everything.

DAY 140:
(May 18)

*Ecclesiastes 11:5-10

"*As you do not know what is the way of the wind, or how the bones grow in the womb . . . so you do not know the works of God who makes everything . . .* Therefore remove sorrow from your heart, and put away evil from your flesh, for childhood and youth are vanity."

We do not know what tomorrow will bring. God has everything in control. There are many mysteries that only God knows. God is the secret to living to the fullest. Trust in the Lord for everything.

DAY 141:
(May 19)

Jeremiah 18:6-15

"O house of Israel, can I not do with you as this potter?" says the Lord. *Because My people have forgotten Me . . . they have caused themselves to stumble in their ways . . . to walk in* pathways and not on a highway."

We serve a mighty God. He is a strong tower. God wants us to obey His commandments to the best of our ability. If we need help in walking the straight and narrow path, let's pray to God for help. He is always available to lead and guide our footsteps.

*Ephesians 1:1-5

Paul, an apostle of Jesus Christ . . . Grace to you and peace from God our Father and the Lord Jesus Christ . . . who has blessed us with every Spiritual blessing in the heavenly places in Christ, *Just as He chose us in Him before the foundation of the world, that we should be holy and without blame before Him in love* . . . according to the good pleasures of His will."

Paul is telling us of the goodness of the Lord. We are God's very own children. Love God and others as you should love yourselves. We were created for God's glory and purpose. Let's pray for a loving heart towards God first, and everyone on the earth.

DAY 143:
(May 21)

*Prayer:

Our Father, who art in heaven, I want to pray today for everyone receiving these morning inspirations. God, touch their hearts, minds, and souls. I pray they will receive Your Holy Spirit. I pray they will get a desire to serve You. Lord I understand Your word is spirit, truth, life, and power that goes about and does what it is You want it to do. I am just a vessel for You, Lord. Continue to give me increase in You to do Your will. Touch each and every person, their families, their health, their finances, their children, and their relationships first with You and with each other. God, give these individuals Your God-kind of Love toward people. Help us all, Lord, to be more like Your Son Jesus. We want to live this life in preparation for eternal life with You, God. Thank You for hearing this prayer, and we will continue to live for You. In Jesus' name we always pray, Amen and Amen again. Thank You, Jesus.

DAY 144:
(May 22)

Matthew 1:18-24

"Now the birth of Jesus Christ was as follows . . . *She will bring forth a Son, and you shall call His name Jesus,* for He shall save His people from their sins . . . *and they shall call His name Immanuel, which is translated, God with us."*

This is the history of the birth of Jesus. This is a true story. Through this information, we are confident that God is always with us. He dwells within us. And He will never leave us because it is His promise to us.

DAY 145:
(May 23)

2 Thessalonians 2:9-17

"The coming of the lawless one is according to the working of Satan, with all power, signs and lying wonders . . . And for this reason God will send them strong delusion, that they should believe the truth but had pleasure in unrighteousness . . . *Therefore brothers and sisters, stand fast and hold the traditions which you were taught.*"

Satan is still alive today as he was in the Bible days. His purpose is to steal, kill, and destroy our lives. The answer to fighting Satan's powers is to get anchored and fastened into God's word. God has promised us protection against all evil if we depend on Him.

DAY 146:
(May 24)

Galatians 5:16-26

"Walk in the Spirit, and you shall not fulfill the lust of the flesh. For the flesh lusts against the Spirit, but if you are led by the Spirit, you are not under the law, *but the fruit of the Spirit is love, joy, peace, longsuffering, kindness, goodness, faithfulness* . . . Gentleness, self-control. Against such there is no law."

We should always walk as if God is watching us. He expects us to live as Jesus did. God has given us free will to operate in a loving way towards our fellow man.

DAY 147:
(May 25)

*Proverbs 16:1-9

"The preparations of the heart belong to man, but the answer of the tongue is from the Lord. *All the ways of man are pure in his own eyes, but the Lord weighs the spirits. Commit your works to the Lord, and your thoughts will be established . . . A man's heart plans his way, but the Lord directs his steps.*"

We all belong to God. He created us in His own image, for His purpose. We should live our lives to please God. Whatever we do, it should be to glorify God.

ΩA

DAY 148:
(May 26)

2 Thessalonians 2:9-17

"The coming of the lawless one is according to the working of Satan, with all power, signs, and lying wonders . . . God will send them strong delusion, that they should believe the lie . . . *Therefore, brethren, stand fast and hold the tradition which you were taught, whether by word or our epistle.*"

Trust God and His word. The Holy Bible tells us everything we need to know about what God expects from us. It teaches us how to live according to His will. Our parents and forefathers laid the foundation; through the word of God, to live a godly life. We should also teach these things to our children.

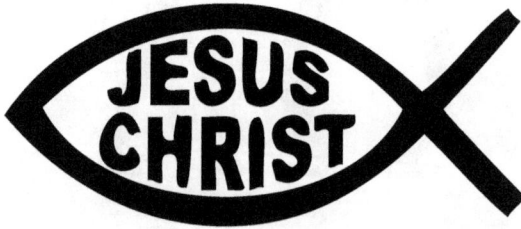

DAY 149:
(May 27)

John 21:18-25

"Most assuredly, I say to you, when you were younger, you girded yourself and walked where you wished; but when you are old, you will stretch out your hands, and others will gird you and carry you where you do not wish . . . *there are also many other things that Jesus did, which if they were written . . . the world . . . could not contain the books that would be written, Amen.*"

Jesus performed many miracles in the sight of the disciples. He challenged Peter to look into his heart and acknowledge who He was. Jesus told Peter to "Feed My sheep." The message given to Peter is the same message for us today.

Hebrews 1:9-14

You have loved righteousness and hated lawlessness . . . And: *"You, Lord, in the beginning laid the foundation of the earth, and the heavens are the work of Your hand. They will perish, but You will remain . . . Are they not all ministering spirits sent forth to minister for those who will inherit salvation?"*

Jesus was sent forth by God, the Father. He was sent to establish the foundation of the world. After doing so, God told Him all these things will perish but He will remain. The angels are ministering spirits which minister to those who will become a part of God's kingdom.

DAY 151:
(May 29)

*1 Peter 3:1-5

"*Wives, submit to your own husbands, that even if they do not obey the word* . . . they may be won by the conduct of their wives . . . Do not let your adornment be merely outward . . . rather let it be the hidden person . . . the holy woman who trusted in God also adorned themselves."

Women are the backbone of a godly family. All eyes are on the woman to show herself as God-fearing. When a man sees his wife being humble and submissive, he can understand how and what God wants from His people. Let's pray for our minds and hearts to be stayed on God.

DAY 152:
(May 30)

*Acts 6:3-7

"Therefore, brethren, seek out from among you seven men of good reputation, full of the Holy Spirit and wisdom, whom we may appoint over our business . . . *But we will give ourselves continually to prayer and to the ministry of the word . . . Then the word of God spread . . .*"

We as children of God need to get into the habit of continually praying for one another. We need to keep God first in everything we do. I believe if we send up a corporate prayer unto God, He will be pleased and grant our request. Let's continue to spread the word of God throughout our generation.

DAY 153:
(May 31)

*Luke 18:1-8

"*Then He spoke a parable to them, that men ought to pray and not lose heart* . . . Now, there was a widow in that city . . . saying, Get justice for me from my adversary . . . Hear what the judge said . . . He will avenge her speedily . . . *when the Son of Man comes, will He find faith on the earth*?"

The widow continually went to the unjust judge for her needs and concerns. God wants us to come to Him daily for our needs. He wants us to pray without ceasing. We should show the same consistency that the widow woman showed.

DAY 154:
(June 1)

*1 Corinthians 15:51-58

"Behold, I tell you a mystery: We shall not all sleep, but we shall be changed. In a moment, in the twinkling of an eye, at the last trumpet, for the trumpet will sound, and the dead will be raised incorruptible . . . But thanks be to God . . . *Therefore, my beloved brethren, be steadfast, immovable, always abounding in the work of the Lord, knowing that your labor is not in vain.*"

The end of time is near. We must continue in the work of the Lord. God promises that we will all be changed if we keep our eyes stayed on Him. Let's continue to pray one for another and be ready when He comes.

*John 1:14-18

"And the Word became flesh and dwelt among us, and we beheld His glory, as of the only begotten of the Father, full of grace and mercy . . . And of His fullness we have all received, and grace to grace . . . *No one has seen God at any time. The only begotten Son, who is in the bosom of the Father, He has declared Him.*"

John the Baptist introduced Jesus to the people upon His arrival. God Himself instructed John the Baptist how to introduce the Son of Man. Jesus is God in the flesh whom no one has ever seen.

DAY 156:
(June 3)

Hebrews 11:1-6

"Now faith is the substance of things hoped for, the evidence of things not seen . . . *But without faith it is impossible to please Him, for who comes to God must believe that He is, and that He is a rewarder of those who diligently seek Him.*"

Anyone, on coming to God, must first believe He exists. God wants people to come to Him with faith that He will hear and answer their prayers. "Let's pray for an increase in our faith!"

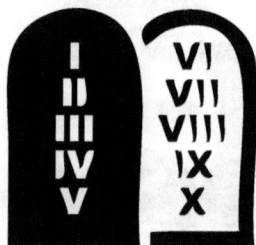

DAY 157:
(June 4)

*2 Corinthians 5:1-10

"For we know if our earthy house, this tent, is destroyed, we have a building from God, a house not made with hands, eternal in the heavens . . . *For we must all appear before the judgment seat of Christ, that each one may receive the things done in the body, according to what he has done, whether good or bad.*"

God promises us a heavenly body after this life if we live according to His will. We need to be careful of the things we do in this earthly body in order to receive the heavenly body. One day we all will be judged.

DAY 158:
(June 5)

Deuteronomy 4:23-31

"Take heed to yourselves, lest you forget the covenant of the Lord . . . which He made with you . . . For the Lord your God is a consuming fire, a jealous God . . . *seek the Lord your God, and you will find Him if you seek Him with your heart and with all your soul* . . . your God is a merciful God."

The Lord has given us the laws (commandments), to follow and live to the best of our ability. He was the same God yesterday as He is today; therefore, we must seek the Lord with our whole hearts, minds, and souls.

Prayer:

God, I say this prayer, in the name of Jesus. I am asking if You would touch our hearts, our minds, and our souls today. God, we need You more today than ever before. We need to know that You exist and that You are real. Pour out Your Holy Spirit upon us today, Lord. Increase our faith in You, Jesus. We want to live according to Your will and purpose for our lives. We don't just want to say we are saved (a child of God), but we want to let Your light shine through us. Give us the heart to show godly love towards one another. We are all the same in Your eyes, Jesus. Let us start being our brother's keeper: giving, loving, and helping one another in times of need. Jesus, it is all about You. You are the beginning and the end, the first and the last, and the Alpha and Omega. I pray today that we will let You, God, be the first and the last thing on our minds everyday from this day forward. I say this prayer in the precious name of our Father and Lord, Jesus Christ, Amen, and Amen again. ("I want to invite everyone to take the time to talk to God every day. He is available and waiting to hear from all of us every day, Thank you!) God bless you all and everyone's entire family.

(June 6)

Genesis 1:26-28

"*Then God said, Let Us make man in Our image, according to Our likeness*; let them have dominion . . . So God created man in His own image . . . male and female He created them."

We are made in the image of God. We need to live according to who we are and how great our Father is. God has given us power and dominion over every other creature He made. We serve a loving God.

(June 7)

Our Father, which art in heaven,
Hallowed be thy name.
Thy kingdom come,
thy will be done, in earth as it is in heaven.
Give us this day our daily bread.
And forgive us our trespasses,
as we forgive them that trespass against us.
And lead us not into temptation;
But deliver us from evil.
For thine is the kingdom,
the Power and the Glory, for ever and ever.
Amen.

(June 8)

The Lord is my shepherd;
I shall not want.
He makes me to lie down in green pastures;
He leads me beside the still waters.
He restores my soul;
He leads me in the paths of righteousness
For His name's sake.
Yea, though I walk through the valley of the shadow of
death, I will fear no evil;
For You are with me;
Your rod and Your staff, they comfort me.
You prepare a table before me
in the presence of my enemies;
You anoint my head with oil;
My cup runs over.
Surely goodness and mercy shall
follow me all the days of my life;
And I will dwell in the house of the Lord Forever.
"Amen!"

DAY 160:
(June 9)

John 20:11-17

"But Mary stood outside the tomb weeping . . . and she saw two angels, one at the head and the other at the feet, where the body of Jesus had lain . . . Jesus said to her, "Woman, why are you weeping . . . I am ascending to My Father and your Father . . . My God and your God.""

Mary witnessed Jesus not being in the tomb. When He appeared to her, He said he was going to be with *our Father* (God). Jesus wants us to understand that we are one with Him and a child of God. He is alive and with us yesterday, today, and forevermore.

DAY 161:
(June 10)

Isaiah 45:18-23

"The Lord created the heavens and formed the earth . . . who formed it to be inhabited: 'I am the Lord, and there is no other' . . .

God is God all by Himself. There is no other god but God the Father. We are to seek after Him with all of our hearts, minds, and souls. Let's pray to God for the will to seek after Him with everything within us.

DAY 162:
(June 11)

Luke 6:40-45

A disciple is not above his teacher, but everyone who is perfectly trained will be like his teacher . . . A good man out of the good treasures of his heart brings forth good . . . *For out of the abundance of the heart his mouth speaks."*

All the ways of man are good in his own eyes, but the Lord weighs the heart and spirit. We need to say what we mean and mean what we say. We should not only talk the talk, but walk the walk. God is watching and listening to everything we say and do.

DAY 163:
(June 12)

*James 4:5-8

"The Spirit who dwells in us yearns jealously. But He gives more grace . . . *God resist(s) the proud, but gives grace to the humble. Therefore submit to God. Resist the devil and he will flee from you. Draw near to God and He will draw near to you.*"

We serve a jealous God. He wants us to be humble in everything we do. We are to do everything in our power to resist negative temptation. Ask God for the strength to draw near to Him and He will help us.

DAY 164:
(June 13)

Proverbs 4:20-27

"My son, give attention to My words; incline your ear to My sayings. Do not let them depart from your ears . . . *Keep your heart with all diligence, for out of it spring the issues of life.*"

God wants us to pay attention to His word. Let's do everything we can to listen for His voice. If we keep our attention on Him, He will bless us totally.

DAY 165:
(June 14)

Galatians 2:15-21

"We who are Jews by nature, and not sinners of the Gentiles, *Knowing that a man is not justified by the works of the law but faith in Jesus Christ* . . . I have been crucified with Christ, it is no longer I who live, but Christ lives in me."

God wants us to do good works, but they alone are not what will get us into the kingdom of heaven. The Bible says when the Son of Man returns, will He find faith on the earth? The main thing God wants us to do is believe in Him.

DAY 166:
(June 15)

*Romans 12:1-3

I beseech you therefore, brethren, by the mercies of God, *that you present your bodies a living sacrifice, holy, acceptable to God, which is your reasonable service.* And do not be conformed to this world, but be transformed by the renewing of your mind."

Our bodies are considered the temple of God. We should live our lives in representation of the Lord. Everything we do; in the body, should be acceptable to God. Every day we should be trying to think and live like Jesus.

DAY 167:
(June 16)

1 Samuel 12:21-25

"And do not turn aside, for then you would go after empty things which cannot profit or deliver, for they are nothing. For the Lord will not forsake His people . . . *Only fear the Lord, and serve Him in truth with all your heart; for consider what great things He has done for you.*"

God wants us to know that we have *free will* to do whatever we wish to do. We have a mind to know right from wrong"; therefore choose wisely. He wants us to remember all the other troubles He has delivered us from, before choosing the wrong path.

DAY 168:
(June 17)

*Matthew 6:1-8

"Take heed that you do not do your charitable deeds before men . . . do not let your left hand know what your right hand is doing . . . *when you pray, go into your room, and when you have shut the door, pray to your Father . . . who knows the things you have need of before you ask."*

We are not to boast in our prayers. God is watching our every move on a daily basis. We only need to come before God in prayer with an open heart. He promises to hear us and help us.

DAY 169:
(June 18)

Isaiah 54:14-17

"In righteousness you shall be established; you shall be far from oppression, for you shall not fear, and from terror, for it shall not come near you . . . *No weapon formed against you shall prosper, and every tongue which rises against in judgment you shall be condemned.*"

God is the author and finisher of everybody and everything. He is the One who created the heavens and the earth. God is the One who allow these weapons to be created. He will protect His people from harm. Let's not be worried or concerned with earthly things. Let's keep our eyes on the Lord.

DAY 170:
(June 19)

*2 Peter 3:7-9

"But the heavens and the earth which now exist are kept in store by the same word, reserved for fire until the Day of Judgment and perdition of ungodly men. *But, beloved, do not forget this one thing, that with the Lord one day is as a thousand years, and a thousand years as one day.* The Lord is not slack concerning His promise . . . that any should perish but that all should come to repentance."

God created the heavens and everything under the heavens. The first earth was destroyed by water. He promises upon the coming of the new earth, everything will be destroyed by fire. Let's get our lives prepared to be with God for eternity.

DAY 171:
(June 20)

*Psalm 139:14-24

"I will praise You, for I am fearfully and wonderfully made; marvelous are Your works . . . *Search me, O God and know my heart; try me, and know my anxieties;* And see if there is any wicked ways in me, and lead me in the way everlasting."

We are made in the image of God. When He made us; He made us for His good and purpose. None of us were born by accident. We should pray and ask God to guide our lives in the path of righteousness. Let's live our lives on earth to live with God everlasting.

DAY 172:
(June 21)

1 John 4:7-12

"Beloved, *let us love one another: for love comes from God; and everyone that loves is born of God, and knows God . . . .*if God loved us, we ought also to love one another. No one has seen God at any time . . . God dwells in us, and his love is perfected in us."

We are expected to love another at all times. God loves us and expects us to love each other. This is our way of showing God's love to the world. We; as Christians, should be an example of God's unconditional love for all mankind.

DAY 173:
(June 22)

*James 1:2-4

"*My brother, count it all joy when ye fall into divers' temptations; knowing this, that the trying of your faith produces patience. But let patience have her perfect work, that ye may be perfect and entire, wanting nothing.*"

When we encounter controversy in our lives, we should look for the opportunity to praise God. He wants us to develop patience, in Him. Faith is what God is looking for in all of us.

DAY 174:
(June 23)

Psalm 118:24

"This is the day that the Lord has made; let us rejoice, and be glad in it."

Let's make today a special day. Let's honor God and know that He has made this day for our enjoyment. Let's not look at the negative, but embrace the positive.

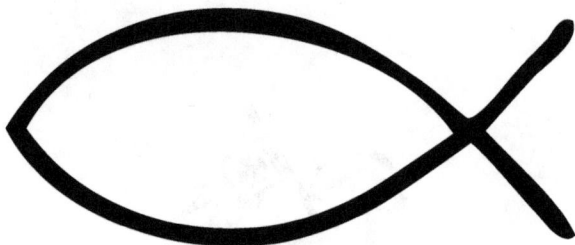

DAY 175:
(June 24)

Matthew 25:20-29

"So he who had received five talents came and brought five other talents, saying, Lord, you delivered me five talents; look, I have gained five more talents besides them. *His lord said to him, well done, good and faithful servant; you were faithful over a few things, I will make you ruler over many things.* Enter into the joy of your Lord."

The Lord has many things in store for us. He wants to see how we will handle a few things. This will determine if He can trust us with many things. We should pray and ask God to teach us His ways and will for our lives.

John 16:29-33

"His disciples said to Him, 'See; now You are speaking plainly, and using no figure of speech!' Indeed the hour is coming . . . *These things I have spoken to you, that in Me you have peace. In the world you will have tribulation; but be of good cheer, I have overcome the world.*"

It was Jesus' time to die on the cross, but He was not afraid. He told the disciples not to worry, but be brave. He warned them that the world will make them suffer, but He would be their strength. Jesus is our help in times of need.

*Psalm 46:1-7

"*God is our refuge and strength, a very present help in trouble. Therefore we will not fear* even though the earth be removed, and though the mountains be carried into the midst of the sea . . . The Lord of host is with us. The God of Jacob is our refuge."

We can depend on our God in every situation. He is always available to show up in our times of need. Tragedy and controversy will affect our lives; but don't look at the problem; look to God. That is where our help comes from.

DAY 178:
(June 27)

*1 Corinthians 3:10-17

"According to the grace of God . . . I have laid the foundation and another build on it. But let each one take heed how he builds on it . . . If anyone's work which he has built on it endures, he will receive a reward . . . *Do you not know that you are the temple of God and that the Spirit of God dwells in you?* If anyone defiles the temple of God, God will destroy him. For the temple of God is holy, which temple are you."

We are the temple of God and God lives within us. We are to treat our bodies as holy because God is holy. What we put in our bodies, we give to God. The way we treat our bodies is the way we treat God. Let's pray that we will keep in mind that we are a representation of Christ Jesus.

DAY 179:
(June 28)

2 Samuel 22:29-33

"For You are my lamp; the Lord shall enlighten my darkness. *As for God, His way is perfect; the word of the Lord is proven; He is a shield to all who trust Him* . . . God is my strength and power and He makes my way perfect."

God wants us to trust Him with all of our concerns and worries. He will protect us from all hurt, harm, and danger. He is a light in a dark place and will guide us through all difficulties. He is our strength when we are weak. God is everything to us.

DAY 180:
(June 29)

*2 Chronicles 7:11-15

"Thus Solomon finished the house of the Lord and the king's house . . . Then the Lord appeared before Solomon by night, and said to him . . . *If My people who are called by My name will humble themselves, and pray and seek My face, and turn from their wicked ways, then I will hear from heaven, and will forgive their sin and heal their land."*

King Solomon wanted to build a temple to please God. Once he got everything and everybody in place and in agreement with him, the Lord appeared. God gave him a very basic, simple instruction. *Pray* together, humble ourselves, and turn from our wickedness—*period.*

DAY 181:
(June 30)

1 Corinthians 14:31-35

"For you call all prophesy one by one, that all may learn and all may be encouraged. And the spirits of the prophets are subject to the prophets. *For God is not the author of confusion but of peace, as in all the churches of the saints.*"

God has put everything and everybody in its place. The prophets are to learn from one another. The churches are subject unto God and God alone. God has assigned whom He wants to speak to His people in and out of the church.

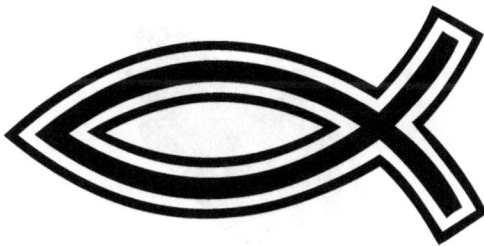

DAY 182:
(July 1)

*Job 22:21-23

"Now acquaint yourself with Him, and be at peace; thereby good wills' come to you. Receive, please, instruction from His mouth, and lay up His word in your heart. If you return to the Almighty, you will be built up; you will remove all iniquity far from your tents."

God wants us to seek after Him. We are to get to know Him on a personal level. The word of God says to seek Him with all of your heart, mind, and soul. Let's pray for a desire to study His word and to seek His face.

DAY 183:
(July 2)

1 John 2:25-29

"And this is the promise that He has promised us—eternal life . . . But the anointing which you have received from Him abides in you . . . And now, little children, *abide in Him, that when He appears, we may have confidence and not be ashamed before Him at His coming."*

If we abide and trust in God, we are promised eternal life. All we have to do is follow His commandments. These are the end of the days we are living in; therefore, we need to prepare ourselves. Make every effort to be acceptable to our God.

Prayer:

Most gracious and holy Father, I come to you with thanksgiving. God, You gave me instructions to write this book on my spiritual journey and quest for You. I thank You, Lord, from the bottom of my heart. These morning inspirations have been a blessing for me as well as others receiving them. Thank You God for my wife, who stuck with me through the rough and hard days it took to stay on task. I look forward to searching the scriptures and learning more and more about You and Your word on a daily basis. Lord, keep me motivated and driven to continue this 365-day spiritual journal. I have made a commitment to write this manuscript for one year. I pray and thank God today for allowing me to reach the half-year mark. Hallelujah! Glory to God! It was only through You that I was able to make it this far. This is my prayer in Jesus' name, Amen.

★Romans 10:8-11

"But what does it say? The word is near you, in your mouth and in your heart (that is the word of faith which we preach): *That if you confess with your mouth the Lord Jesus and believe in your heart that God has raised Him from the dead, you will be saved."*

Salvation is already in all of us. We just need to activate it. To get closer to God, all we have to do is believe: believe that Jesus died for our sins and God raised Him from the dead. Let's activate our faith today.

DAY 185:
(July 4)

John 6:4-14

"Now the Passover, a feast of the Jews, was near . . . *There is a lad here who has five barley loaves and two small fish . . . Then Jesus said, Make the people sit down . . . And Jesus took the loaves, and when He had given thanks He gave them to the disciples . . . So when they were filled, He said . . . Gather up the fragments that remain . . .* Then those men, when they had seen the sign that Jesus did, said, This is truly the Prophet who is to come onto the world."

Jesus performed signs and miracles in the presence of His disciples. They many times forgot about them, but this was a memorable moment. Jesus fed five thousand people with five loaves of bread and two fish. Amazing!

DAY 186:
(July 5)

Hebrews 13:1-3

"*Let brotherly love continue. Do not forget to entertain strangers, for by so doing some have unwittingly entertained angels.* Remember the prisoners as if chained with them—those who are mistreated—since you yourselves are in the body also."

We should treat other as we want to be treated. God lets us know that we are *one* in Him. Everyone is the same in God's eyes. Let's do unto others as we would have them do unto us.

DAY 187:
(July 6)

Ephesians 1:3-12

"Blessed be the God and Father of our Lord Jesus Christ, who has blessed us with every spiritual blessing in the heavenly places in Christ . . . *In Him also we have obtained an inheritance, being predestined according to the purpose of Him who works all things according to the counsel of His will.*"

God has already imparted in us the spiritual gifts we need. We are His sons and daughters; therefore, we have His promise of eternal life. We need to let go and let God have His way in us to fulfill His purpose.

DAY 188:
(July 7)

*Ecclesiastes 7:16-20

"*Do not be overly righteous, nor be foolish:* Why should you die before your time? Wisdom strengthens the wise . . . *For there is not a just man on earth who does good and does not sin.*"

Anyone who thinks he knows everything about God and His ways is a fool. We all have things to learn and need to continue to seek the wisdom of God. We all have fallen short to be righteous in God's eyes.

DAY 189:
(July 8)

Proverbs 30:5-6

"*Every word of God is pure; He is a shield to those who put their trust in Him. Do not add to His words*, lest he rebuke you, and you be found a liar."

God's word is the truth. They are the direct words from God Himself. God wants us to put our trust in Him and Him alone. He does not want us to add or subtract anything from His word. Let's pray to keep God's words to only what they say in the Bible.

Prayer:

Heavenly Father, Forgive me this day for falling behind in my quest to write this book. I fell behind three days without ever realizing it. I sent the morning inspirations out on my cell phone, but did not write them in the manuscript. Lord help me to stay on task. Help me to have the desire and drive to complete the 365 days I promised to You. Lord, give me the strength to continue to write what You want me to send out daily. I love you God, and I thank You for giving me this assignment. I pray this prayer in Jesus' name, Amen.

DAY 189:
(July 9)

***Psalm 91:8-11**

"Only with your eyes shall you look, and see the reward of the wicked. Because you have made the Lord, who is my refuge . . . your dwelling place, No evil shall befall you . . . *For he shall give His angels charge over you, to keep you in all your ways* . . . In their hands, they shall bear you up."

God will show us the things He has in store for those who do follow Him. He will allow His angels to protect us and hide us from all harm. It is up to us to live right for God.

DAY 190:
(July 10)

Galatians 5:19-26

"Now the works of the flesh are evident . . . *And those who are Christ's have crucified the flesh with its passions and desires. If we live in the Spirit, let us walk in the Spirit. Let us not become conceited, provoking one another, envying one another.*"

We should examine ourselves to see that we are truly walking with God. If we are passionate about the Lord, we will crucify our flesh and live in the Spirit. Let's began to show brotherly love towards one another.

DAY 191:
(July 11)

*Ephesians 1:14-19

"Who is the guarantee of our inheritance until the redemption of the praise of His glory . . . *Do not cease to give thanks for you; making mention of you in my prayers:* The eyes of your understanding being enlightened . . ."

Continue to seek after Him and continue to praise His Holy name. Pray and ask God to empower you with His Holy Spirit, that you might know Him better. If you want God's knowledge and wisdom, ask Him.

DAY 192:
(July 12)

Ecclesiastes 9:10-12

"*Whatever your hand finds to do, do it with all your' might;* for there is no work or device or knowledge or wisdom in the grave where you are going. *The race is not to the swift, nor does the battle to the strong . . . but time and chance happen to them all.*"

God wants us to do whatever we do as if unto Him. He is the author and finisher of our fate. We should do our daily chores in a godly manner. Remember God has His eyes in every place. Nothing we do is hidden from Him.

Ephesians 4:4-7

"There is one body and one Spirit, just as you were called to one hope of your calling; One Lord, one faith, one baptism; One God and Father of all, and in you all."

God chose each one of us to become a part of His kingdom. There is only one of us and one God. The Holy Spirit of God dwells in all of us. There is one God, one Lord, and Savior, Jesus Christ. We all have the spirit of the living God inside of us.

DAY 194:
(July 14)

1 John 5:11-15

"And this is the testimony: that God has given us eternal life, and this life is in His Son. He who has the Son has life . . . *Now this is the confidence that we have in Him, that if we ask anything according to His will, He hears us . . ."*

Our hope for eternal life; lies in our belief in God's Son, Jesus Christ. When we believe in Jesus, we believe in life after death. Jesus is our gateway to God. Our prayers go through Jesus; directly to God, the Father.

DAY 195:
(July 15)

*James 3:5-10

"*Even so the tongue is a little member* and boasts great things. See how great a forest a little fire kindles! The tongue is a fire . . . The tongue is set among our members that it defiles the whole body . . . *But no man can tame the tongue. It is an unruly evil; full of deadly poison* . . . Out of the same mouth precedes blessing and cursing."

We ought to watch what comes out of our mouth. Although the tongue is a small member of the body, it carries a lot of weight. People are helped or hurt through the words we say to them. Let's pray for God to renew the right spirit in us, to only bless the ones we come in contact with.

DAY 196:
(July 16)

Matthew 23:11-12

"But he who is greatest among you shall be your servant. *And whoever exalts himself will be humbled, and he who humbles himself will be exalted."*

God wants us to be servants. There is none of us greater than the other, in God's eyes. People put titles on their names to lift themselves up. God will humble them and exalt the humbled.

Prayer:

Thank you, Jesus, for enlarging my territory. This weekend I was allowed to add more names to the morning inspiration list. As of today, I am spreading God's word to many more people. (God is good). Help me Lord as I continue to send out Your word daily. If it is Your will, I am ready to add more people to this list. Thank You again, in Jesus name, Amen.

DAY 197:
(July 17)

Philippians 2:13-16

"*For it is God who works in you both to will and to do His good pleasures . . . Do all things without complaining and disputing. That you may become blameless and harmless . . . Holding fast to the word of life . . .*"

All the things we do, we shall do unto God. It is God whom we should try to please. We are living in the last days; therefore let's live life differently than the world. Let's follow the Lord's commandments.

DAY 198:
(July 18)

*Hebrews 11:1-6

"Now faith is the substance of things hoped for, the evidence of things not seen . . . *But without faith it is impossible to please Him, for he who comes to God must believe that He is,* and that He is a rewarder of those who diligently seek Him."

We serve an awesome God. All He expects us to do is Believe that He exist. We can ask God of anything, and He will hear us and help us. All God wants us to do is have "*Faith*" and believe in what you ask Him for.

DAY 199:
(July 19)

Romans 14:10-13

"But why do you judge your brother? *For we shall all stand before the judgment seat of Christ . . . So then each of us shall give an account of himself to God.* Therefore let us not judge one another anymore . . ."

We have no right to judge one another. Our concern should be how we can please God for ourselves. When we stand before God; we will have to give an account for what we have done, not anyone else.

DAY 200:
(July 20)

Psalm 53:1-3

"The fool has said in his heart, 'There is no God'. They are corrupt . . . there is none who does good . . . *God looks down from heaven upon the children of men, to see if there are any who understand, who seek God.*"

God is paying attention to our actions and our ways. We will have to give an account to God at the judgment. Let's pray and ask God to help us walk in the way He wants us to.

DAY 201:
(July 21)

Philippians 4:4-8

"Rejoice in the Lord always. Again I will say, rejoice! *Be anxious for nothing, but in everything by prayer and supplication, with thanksgiving, let your request be known to God;* and the peace of God, which surpasses all understanding, will guard your hearts and minds. . ."

First, we should give thanks to God in all things. Rejoice and be content with the fact that God's will is being done. If anyone has a request or need from the Lord, he should bring it to Him through prayer. Our God looks at the heart of man. Pray and believe your prayer will be answered.

DAY 202:
(July 22)

Luke 15:4-7

"What man of you, having a hundred sheep, if he loses one of them, does he leave the ninety-nine in the wilderness, and go after the one which is lost until he finds it? *I say to you that likewise there will be more joy in heaven over one sinner who repents than over ninety-nine just persons who need no repentance."*

God loves all of His creation. He loves the ones who have not yet come to Him. Therefore, when a sinner decides to repent and come to God, He orders a celebration in heaven. The angels welcome them unto God with song and praise. What a wonderful celebration, for one of God's children to come to Christ..

DAY 203:
(July 23)

*1 Peter 4:5-10

"They will give an account to Him who is ready to judge the living and the dead . . . But the end of all things is at hand; *therefore be serious and watchful in your prayers. And above all things have fervent love for one another, for love will cover a multitude of sins.* As each one has received a gift, minister it to one another . . ."

We are living in the end of time. It is time to get serious with ourselves and God. We are instructed to love our neighbors as ourselves. Let's pray for a heart to love all people.

DAY 204:
(July 24)

Philippians 3:13-17

"Brethren, I do not count myself to have apprehended; but one thing I do, *forgetting those things which are behind and reaching forward to those things which are ahead, I press towards the goal for the prize of the upward call of God in Christ Jesus . . .*"

Let us live in Christ Jesus. He is the one to order our footsteps. Our responsibility is to press forward to reach our calling in Him. Forget about the past and concentrate on the future.

DAY 205:
(July 25)

*Matthew 6:5-8

"And when you pray, you shall not be like the hypocrites. For they love to pray standing in the synagogues and on the corner streets . . . *But when you pray, go into your room, and when you have shut your door,* pray to your Father who is in the secret place . . . *For your Father knows the things you have need of before you ask Him."*

Many people pray so others can hear them. They broadcast their prayer requests so others can see that they are religious. God wants us to go into a secret place and pray to Him in private. He wants a one-on-one relationship with us. He already knows what we need before we even ask. Let's not pray like the world, but as Jesus has instructed us to do.

DAY 206:
(July 26)

Ephesians 2:1-10

"And you He made alive, who were dead in transgression and sins, in which you once walked . . . we all once conducted ourselves in the lust of our flesh . . . But God, who is rich in mercy . . . *For we are His workmanship, created in Christ Jesus for good works, which God prepared beforehand that we should walk in them.*"

We all once walked contrary to God. While living a life without Jesus, God still had His hands on us. He loved us even in our messy lifestyle. God's mercy and grace reached out and saved us. Before we were born, God already had us on His mind. He had a plan for us to follow Him and lead others to Him.

Romans 14:10-13

"But why do you judge your brother? *For it is written, 'As I live, says the Lord, every knee shall bow to Me, and every tongue shall confess to God.'* Therefore let us not judge one another anymore."

Many of us have the habit of judging our fellow man. God tells us not to judge one another. God is the only One we will need to stand in front of in judgment. We will all one day have to bow down to Jesus and confess our sins to God.

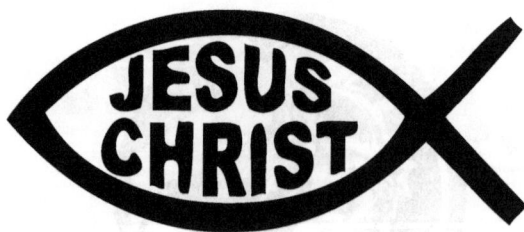

*_James 1:19-24_

"_So then, my beloved, let every man be swift to hear, slow to speak, slow to wrath_ . . . But be doers of the word, and not hearers only, deceiving yourselves . . .

We should all be quick to listen and slow to speak. It is not Christ-like to get angry easily. God wants us to do as the word tells us to do. When we ignore what God tells us to do, we are not being true to ourselves. Let's pray for a heart and mind to serve God with everything we have.

ΩA

DAY 209:
(July 29)

1 John 4:13-21

"By this we know that we abide in Him, and He in us, because He has given us His Spirit . . . We love Him because He first loved us . . . If anyone says, 'I love God,' and hates his brother, he is a liar; *for he who does not love his brother whom he has seen, how can he love God whom he has not seen . . . he who loves God must love his brother also."*

We are made in the image of God. God wants us to be like His Son Jesus. Jesus is love. Our brothers and sisters are all men and women in the world. This means the saved and the unsaved. We prove our love to God by loving our brothers and sisters. Let's ask God to give us godlike love toward all human beings.

*1 Corinthians 10:12-13

"Therefore let him who thinks he stands alone take heed lest he fall. No temptation has overtaken you except such as is common to man; but *God is faithful, who will not allow you to be tempted beyond what you are able* . . . that you will be able to bear it."

Temptations are bound to come. He has given us free will to do as we please. We should always take God into consideration before making descisions. Let's keep God *first* in everything we say, think, and do.

DAY 211:
(July 31)

John 3:12-19

"If I have told you earthly things and you do not believe, how will you believe if I tell you heavenly things . . . *For God so loved the world that He gave His only begotten Son, that whoever believes in Him should not perish but have everlasting life* . . . He who believes in Him is not condemned . . ."

God loves us so much He sacrificed His only Son to die, so that we might have eternal life. God has great love for His creation. He wants everyone to be saved so we can live with Him forever. His will is that all mankind enter into eternal life with Him.

DAY 212:
(August 1)

*Luke 6:39-42

"And He spoke a parable to them: 'Can the blind lead the blind?' Will they both fall into the ditch? A disciple is not above his teacher . . . *And why do you look at the speck in your brother's eye, but do not perceive the plank in your own eye. . .*Hypocrite! First remove the plank in your own eye, then you will see clearly to remove the speck that is in your brother's eye."

We are quick to judge one another. God says we need to clean up our own stuff before we begin to try and lead someone else towards Him. He expects us to be as clean as our brother. We all have issues, situations, and problems in our lives, which will affect our spiritual growth. Let's pray to God for every area of our lives we need help in.

DAY 213:
(August 2)

1 Peter 2:7-10

"Therefore, to you who believe, He is precious; but those who are disobedient, 'the stone which the builders rejected has become the chief cornerstone . . . *But you are a chosen generation, a royal priesthood, a holy nation, His own special people . . .*"

God loves us so much; He made us higher than all other created things. He made us in His own image. They rejected Jesus, but He is a strong foundation to all mankind. We are His people and He is our God.

DAY 214:
(August 3)

*Psalm 27:10-14

"When my mother and father forsake me, then the Lord will take care of me. Teach me Your way, O Lord, and lead me in a smooth path . . . Do not deliver me to the will of my adversaries . . . *Wait on the Lord; be of good courage, and he shall strengthen your heart, wait, I say, on the Lord.*"

The Lord is our strength when we don't have anyone else to depend on. He will hide and protect us from our enemies. God only asks that we will *wait* upon Him to deliver us. Some things God want us to experience to make us strong. He wants us to depend on Him for our deliverance.

DAY 215:
(August 4)

*Mark 12:28-31

"Then one of the scribes came . . . ask Him, 'Which is the first commandment of all?' Jesus answered him, 'the first of all the commandments is: the Lord is one. *And you shall love the Lord your God with all your heart, with all your soul, with all your mind, and with all your strength, this is the first commandment.* And the second is . . . You shall love your neighbor as yourself."

Of all the commandments, God wants us to *love.* God wants us to have a god-like love toward Him and everyone else. He commands us to love Him with everything within us. Love Him with every fiber in our body. He wants us to feel love towards Him with great passion.

DAY 216:
(August 5)

Deuteronomy 5:16-22

"Honor your father and mother, as the Lord your God has commanded you, that your days may be long, and that it will be well with you in the land which the Lord your God is giving you. You shall not murder. You shall not commit adultery. You shall not steal . . . These words the Lord spoke to the assembly, in the mountain . . ."

God has laid out specific rules for us to follow. He set in place the law, which we are to obey. These rules are *The Ten Commandments*. God said if we love Him, we will follow these commandments. They should come easy for those who have their faith in Him.

DAY 217:
(August 6)

2 Corinthians 5:16-18

"Therefore, from now on, we regard no one according to the flesh. Even though we have known Christ according to the flesh . . . *Therefore, if anyone is in Christ, he is a new creation; old things have passed away; behold, all things have become new.* Now all things are from God . . .

Before we gave our lives to Christ, we lived a sinful life. We did everything that we were big and bad enough to do. Once we give our lives to God, we become new creatures; a new creation. All of the past is in the past, and we begin to live a new life. We should be living our lives for God.

DAY 218:
(August 7)

1 Peter 3:8-14

"Finally, all of you be of one mind having compassion for another; love as brothers be tenderhearted and courteous; not returning evil for evil . . . *For He who would love life and see good days, let him refrain his tongue from evil . . .* Let him turn away from evil and do good . . . *For the eyes of the Lord are on the righteous, and His ears are open to his prayers . . .*"

God wants us to all be in one accord. He wants us to love one another as we should love ourselves. If we love God, we should love each other. We should turn away from doing anything that is against God. Let's pray to have the same mind as God and to love one another with genuine love.

DAY 219:
(August 8)

Isaiah 40:28-31

"Have you not known? Have you not heard? The everlasting God, the Lord, the Creator of the ends of the earth, neither faints nor is weary. His understanding is unsearchable. *He gives power to the weak, and to those who have no might He increases strength* . . . But those who wait on the Lord shall renew their strength; they shall mount up with wings like eagles, they shall run and not be weary, they shall walk and not faint.'

God is our all-knowing, all-powerful Father. He has all power in His hands. He is unstoppable and immovable. He is in control of us and gives generously to His children. If anyone has a need, they should go to God and ask. When you ask, believe with your whole heart. He will supply all of our needs. When we are weak, He is always there to help us through.

DAY 220:
(August 9)

*_James 4:6-8_

"God resists the proud, but gives grace to the humble. _Therefore submit to God. Resist the devil and he will flee from you. Draw near to God and He will draw near to you._"

God wants us to be humble. Anyone who is proud should seek after God for direction. He will humble you and make you strong. Whenever the devil tries to attack you, ask God for His power to resist him. God is always available.

DAY 221:
(August 10)

Proverbs 22:2-6

"The rich and the poor have this in common; the Lord is the maker of them all. By humility and the fear of the Lord are riches and honor and life . . . *Train up a child in the way he should go; and when he is old he will not depart from it.*"

God has made all people in His image. We are His special creation. Whether rich or poor, He loves us all the same. We as adults and parents are required to teach our children about our Father, Jesus Christ. God expects us to spread His good news to all people.

DAY 222:
(August 11)

Hebrews 2:1-4

"*Therefore we must give the most earnest heed to the things we have heard, lest we drift away.* How shall we escape if we neglect so great a salvation ... God also bearing witness both with signs and wonders, with various miracles, and gifts of the Holy Spirit, according to His own will."

God is telling us to hold onto the messages that are taught to us through His angels. God put certain people in our lives to minister to us. We must pay careful attention to listen, hold onto, and take heed to these things. God has sent His Holy Spirit to help us stay close to Him.

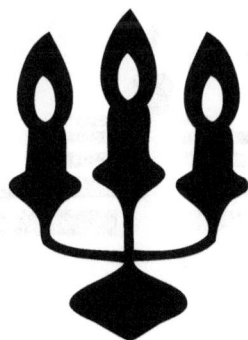

*Philippians 2:2-5

"Fulfill my joy by being like-minded, having the same love, being of one accord, of one mind. *Let nothing be done through selfish ambition or conceit, but in lowliness of mind let each esteem others better than himself* . . . Let this mind be in you which was also in Christ Jesus."

We are to think and act like Jesus. Our goal is to continue to be more like Jesus. Jesus should be our example of how to live and how to treat others. God has His eyes on us twenty-four hours a day; seven days a week. Let's pray for a heart and mind to follow Jesus' example.

DAY 224:
(August 13)

Matthew 26:41

"Watch and pray so that you will not fall into temptation. The spirit is willing, but the flesh is weak."

We need to always be praying for our strength in Christ Jesus. His word says to pray without ceasing. We ought to be praying for every situation pertaining to our lives. Let's continue to ask God to increase our prayer life and always come to Him for everything.

Prayer:

Today I come to You, Lord, to first say "Thank you." Lord I am forever grateful that You have allowed me to continue this book. Father, in the name of Jesus, I thank You. As of today, You have enlarged my territory—Hallelujah. Lord, I could not have done this on my own. Continue to be with me daily as I search Your word to find the morning messages. I say this prayer, and all my prayers, in Jesus' name, Amen.

DAY 225:
(August 14)

*Acts 2:36-39

"Therefore let all the house of Israel know assuredly that God has made Jesus, whom you crucified both Lord and Christ . . . Men and brethren, what shall we do? Then Peter said, *Repent, and let every one of you be baptized in the name of Jesus Christ for the remission of sins; and you shall receive the gift of the Holy Spirit.* For the promise is for you and your children . . ."

God has made a promise to us that we can enter into His kingdom thru repentance. All we have to do is follow His Ten Commandments. God is standing at the door waiting for us to knock.

DAY 226:
(August 15)

*1 John 4:1-6

"Beloved, do not believe every spirit, but test the spirits, whether they are of God; because many false prophets have gone out into the world . . . every spirit that does not confess that Jesus Christ has come in the flesh is not of God . . . *You are of God, little children . . . because He who is in you is greater than he who is in the world . . .*"

There will be many false prophets coming in the name of Jesus to try and deceive us. God warns us that we can spot them by their testimonies. If they do not believe that Jesus is our Lord and Savior do not follow them. They will speak of things of the world, but we, the children of God, will speak things of God.

DAY 227:
(August 16)

*1 Peter 5:5-10

"Likewise you younger people, submit yourselves to your elder . . . Therefore humble yourselves under the mighty hand of God, that He may exalt you in due time . . . *Be sober, be vigilant; because your adversary the devil walks about like a roaring lion, seeking whom he may devour . . .*"

We need to listen to the older saints of God. They tend to have the knowledge and wisdom that will keep us focused on God. The devil is constantly out to destroy God's kingdom. The people of God should always be on guard to pray to God for His protection from evil.

DAY 228:
(August 17)

Ecclesiastes 5:2-6

Do not be rash with your mouth, and let thine heart be hasty to utter anything before God. For God is in heaven, and you are on earth; therefore let your words be few . . . *When you make a vow to God, do not delay to pay it . . . Pay what you have vowed.* Better not to vow than to vow and not pay."

God is always watching and paying attention to us. We tend to make promises to God in order to get out of trouble. God's word says, do not make a vow and go back on your word. There are consequences to telling God a lie. Let's be very careful how we come before God and not go back on our word.

DAY 229:
(August 18)

*Luke 12:2-3

"For there is nothing covered that will not be revealed, nor hidden that will not be known. Therefore whatever you have spoken in the dark will be heard in the light."

God has eyes in every place. He knows our coming in and going out. He also knows our thoughts. God is so powerful and great; He knows what we are in need of before we ask. Therefore, we should keep our minds, hearts, and souls focused on God at all times. He listens to our hearts.

DAY 230:
(August 19)

*Colossians 3:1-14

"If then you were raised with Christ, seek those things which are above, where Christ is, sitting at the right hand of God. *Set your minds on things above, not on things on the earth . . .* But above all these things put on love."

Now that we are children of God; we need to practice what we preach and pay special attention to how we live. We need to have a desire to be like Jesus. Let us have the mind of Christ and above all things, *love.*

Titus 3:3-11

"For we ourselves were also once foolish, disobedient, serving various lusts and pleasures . . . But when the kindness and the love of God our Savior towards man appeared . . . He saved us . . . *But avoid foolish disputes, genealogies, contentions, and strivings about the law; for they are unprofitable and useless.*"

We are going to run into people who think they know more about the Bible and God than we do. The Bible tells us to confront them only twice; then after the second time, have nothing to do with them. Avoid being caught in an argument or quarrel with these kinds of people. They will be self-condemned.

DAY 232:
(August 21)

Romans 15:1-7

"We who are strong ought to bear with the scruples of the weak, and not to please ourselves. Let each of us please his neighbor . . . *For whatever things were written before were written for our learning, that we through the patience and comfort of the Scriptures might have hope . . .* Therefore receive one another just as Christ received us, to the glory of God."

We are of one body in Christ Jesus. God wants us to help one another in the faith. If one is weak, we are to lift them up. We should pass on everything we learn of God to someone else. Let's pray to God and ask for the heart to teach and or preach His word.

DAY 233:
(August 22)

1 Corinthians 2:9-11

"But as it is written: '*Eyes has not seen, nor ear heard, nor have entered into the heart of man the things which God has prepared for those who love Him.*' For what man knows the things of a man except the spirit of the man which is in him? Even so no one knows the things of God except the Spirit of God."

God loves us so much; it is impossible to comprehend the extent of it. Our thoughts cannot think of the amount of love God has for us. He also loves us unconditionally. He wants us to show the love He has towards us to others we come in contact with. Let's show god-like love to everyone.

DAY 234:
(August 23)

Ephesians 6:7-8

"*With good will doing service, as to the Lord, and not to men,* knowing that whatever good anyone does, he will receive the same from the Lord, whether he is a slave or free.

Whatever we do in this life; let's do it with all of our might, as if God is watching us. We always want to be pleasing to God, at all times. I truly believe this is how we live a god-like life. It builds the character personality that promotes real, true, genuine love towards people.

DAY 235:
(August 24)

1 Peter 4:7-11

"The end of all things is near. Therefore be alert and of sober mind so that you may pray. Above all, love each other deeply; because love covers a multitude of sins . . . *Each of you should use whatever gifts you have received to serve others, as faithful stewards of God's grace in various forms* . . . To Him be the glory and the power for ever and ever, Amen.

The end of time is drawing near. It's time to get serious about our relationship with God. We can see all the things being fulfilled that are referenced in the bible. Let's open our eyes and our minds to be ready when He returns.

DAY 236:
(August 25)

Matthew 7:21-23

"*Not everyone who says to Me, 'Lord, Lord,' shall enter the kingdom of heaven, but he who does the will of My Father in heaven* . . . And then I will declare to them, 'I never knew you; depart from Me.*"*

The word of God is nothing to play with. Many people are living a religious lifestyle, but are not creating a personal relationship with God. We should learn to not just talk about God's business, but be about it.

DAY 237:
(August 26)

*James 1:2-8

"My brethren, count it all joy when you fall into various trials, knowing that the testing of your faith produces patience. But let patience have its perfect work, that you may be perfect and complete, lacking nothing . . ."

We will all face trials in our lives. God wants to see how we stand or fall during troubling times. We are to put our total trust in the Lord in every situation. Ask God to help you through any challenges you need help with. He is always available and ready to show up.

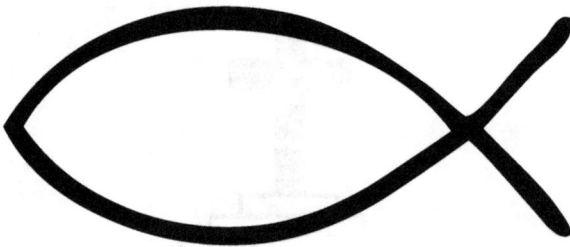

DAY 238:
(August 27)

*Deuteronomy 4:2

"You shall not add to the word which I command you, nor take from it, that you may keep the commandments of the Lord your God which I command you."

We shall not add or subtract to the word of God. God is the author of the Bible and His word is truth. Many people sometimes interrupt or change the words in the Bible to fit their lifestyle. God commands us to simply obey His commandments.

Prayer:

Most Holy and gracious God, continue to pour out Your spirit upon Your people. Your word is truth and people are turning towards You through these, Your morning inspirations. God, I thank You for increasing the number receiving these messages to almost fifty people. "Hallelujah, glory to God!" My prayer today is that each individual receiving Your word has a supernatural breakthrough. Bless them, Lord, and heal them. Give them the desires of their hearts. I say this prayer, in Jesus' name, Amen and Amen again!

DAY 239:
(August 28)

Joshua 1:7-9

"Only be strong and very courageous, that you may observe to do according to all of the law which Moses My servant commanded you; do not turn from it to the right hand or to the left, that you may prosper wherever you go. *This Book of the Law shall not depart from your mouth, but you shall meditate in it day and night* . . . for the Lord your God is with you wherever you go."

We need to take the word of God seriously. Be strong and stand on it. The word is God and God is the word. We ought to study it on a daily basis and learn it from cover to cover. Whenever we speak, it should have something to do with the goodness of God. He is our source and our everything.

DAY 240:
(August 29)

Psalm 37:22-25

"For those blessed by Him shall inherit the earth, but those cursed by Him shall be cut off. *The steps of a good man are ordered by the Lord, and He delights in his way.* Though he falls, he shall not be utterly cast down . . ."

God pays special attention to His children. Those of us who pay attention to His laws are inherited into His kingdom. God wants us all to follow His ways. He will order our steps and protect us when we run into trouble. We should depend on God to direct our paths.

DAY 241:
(August 30)

Jeremiah 1:4-5

"The word of the Lord came to me saying, *'Before I formed you in the womb I knew you; before you were born I sanctified you'; I ordained you as a prophet to the nation.*"

We are made in the image of God. He is the potter and we are the clay. He had us in mind before the foundation of the world. Every one of us was made to do the will of God. Jesus stands at the door waiting for us to knock. We are His vessels to lead others to Him. It's time to activate our gifts.

DAY 242:
(August 31)

Mark 9:17-29

"Then one of the crowd answered and said, 'Teacher, I brought You my son, who has a mute spirit' . . . so I spoke to Your disciples that they should cast it out, but they could not. He answered and said, 'O faithless generation' . . . Jesus said to him, *'If you can believe, all things are possible to him who believes'* . . . This kind can come out of nothing but prayer and fasting."

Jesus performed many signs, wonders, and miracles. He cast out demons, opened blind eyes and healed the sick, just to name a few. Jesus let us know that we can do these same types of things, but we must first have faith. We must also be in continual prayer and fast whenever possible. Let's pray for the power to perform signs, wonders, and miracles like in the Bible days.

Ephesians 4:25-32

"Therefore putting away lying, 'Let each one of you speak truth with his neighbor,' for we are members of one another. *Be angry, and do not sin: do not let the sun go down on your wrath, nor give place to the devil . . . And be kind to one another . . . even as God . . . forgave you.*"

It is time to get serious about God and the way we are living. By now, we should know what not to do. We should know not to lie, not to steal, not to kill, or do the things that are against the Ten Commandments. Always strive to have peace in your heart before going to bed. It is best to rest in peace and harmony with God, so we can rise with love in our hearts.

DAY 244:
(September 2)

*Hebrews 12:1-3

"Therefore we also, since we are surrounded by so great a cloud of witnesses, *let us lay aside every weight, and the sin which so easily ensnares us, and let us run with endurance the race that is set before us ...*"

There are a great number of people in the world that believe in our Lord and Savior, Jesus Christ. We believe that God sent His only begotten Son, Jesus, to come down to earth and die for our sins. It is time to forget about the small things in life, which are holding us back from serving God, and press forward towards loving and living in God.

September 2, I became ordained as an Elder of the church. This is such an honor and privilege to represent the church. I promise to let God have His way in my life and use me for His glory. Whatever assignment He lays before me, I will perform it in Jesus' name. I am already representing the church by providing pastoral care at the hospital as the chaplain. I look forward to seeing what God has in store for me. I want to thank God again, and I give Him my life, heart, mind, and soul.

Prayer: *Hallelujah, Glory to God. I magnify You today, Lord. You are my strength and my salvation. I love You, God, with all of my heart. If it had not been for You on my side, I don't know where I would be today. So I thank You. Lord, You are the King of Kings, the Lord of Lords, the Beginning and the End, the First and Last. You are Alpha and Omega, the Bright and Morning Star, and the Lilly in the Valley. You, Lord, are everything to me. I promise to serve You for the rest of my life. I say this prayer, and all prayers, in Jesus' almighty name, Amen, and Amen again.*

DAY 245:
(September 3)

*Isaiah 53:4-6

"Surely He has borne our grief and carried our sorrows; yet we esteemed Him . . . *But He was wounded for our transgressions, He was bruised for our iniquities; the chastisement for our peace was upon Him, and by His stripes we are healed.* All we like sheep has gone astray . . ."

Jesus died for all of us. He was raised on the third day. He died for our sins; that we might live with Him forever. He was beaten and bruised and now sits at the right-hand of God, the Father, in heaven. He only asks that we serve and love Him until He returns.

DAY 246:
(September 4)

Matthew 19:13-15

"Then people brought little children to Jesus for Him to place His hands on them and pray for them. But the disciples rebuked them. *Jesus said, 'Let the little children come to Me, and do not hinder them, for the kingdom of heaven belongs to such as these . . .'*"

Jesus has a special love for His children. He wants us to humble ourselves as little children. As we do, we will be more eager, willing, and excited about learning more about Him. Let's get serious about our relationship with God.

DAY 247:
(September 5)

*Galatians 6:7-10

"Do not be deceived: God cannot be mocked. A man reaps what he sows . . . *Let us not become weary in doing good, for at the proper time we will reap a harvest if we do not give up. Therefore, as we have* opportunity let us do good to all people, especially to those who belong to the family of believers."

We can fool some of the people sometimes; but we can *never* fool God. He knows our laying down and knows when we rise. He made us and knows our hearts. He wants us to hang in there with Him until the end. We will reap a harvest when Jesus returns.

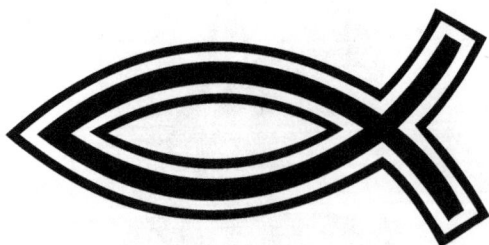

DAY 248:
(September 6)

James 5:19-20

"*My Brothers and sisters, if one of you should wander from the truth and someone should bring that person back,* remember this: *Whoever turns a sinner from the error of their way will save them from death* and cover a multitude of sins."

Many of us will become weary and feel that this walk is in vain. We may even feel like giving up and deciding to return to a life of sin. God wants us to help each other to stay on track. We are our brother's keeper. The word of God says to sin is death. Let's mentor each other and look for life after death.

DAY 249:
(September 7)

Matthew 16:23-24

"Jesus turned and said to Peter, 'Get behind Me, Satan! You are a stumbling block to me' . . . Then Jesus said to His disciples, *'Whoever wants to be My disciples must deny themselves and take up their cross and follow Me.* For whoever wants to save their life will lose it, but whoever loses their life for Me will find it."

God wants us to forget about ourselves and be concerned about others. Once we know who God is and what He can do, we need to lead others to Him. We deny ourselves because we know God is the One who takes care of us. So, to lose your life for God is to find eternal life with Christ.

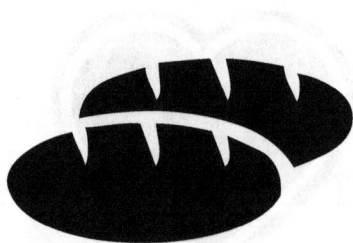

DAY 250:
(September 8)

*Proverbs 3:3-8

"Let love and faithfulness never leave you; bind them around your neck, write them on the tablet of your heart . . . *Trust in the Lord with all your heart and lean not to your own understanding; in all your ways submit to him,* and he will make your path straight . . ."

God is love. God wants us to put love in our hearts. In all our ways and in everything we do; let it be in love. God will be a part of everything that has to do love. Let's pray to become more lovable.

DAY 251:
(September 9)

Ephesians 1:3-8

"Praise be to the God and Father of our Lord Jesus Christ, who has blessed us in the heavenly realms with every spiritual blessing in Christ. *For He chose us before the creation of the world to be holy and blameless in His sight* . . . In Him we have redemption . . . in accordance with the riches of God's grace."

God knew us before we were born. He created us in His image and likeness. He made sure we had all of the spiritual gifts we need to commune with Him. There is no blessing that God doesn't want us to have. He just wants us to love and depend on Him for everything.

DAY 252:
(September 10)

1 Timothy 6:1-10

"These are the things you are to teach and insist on . . . godliness with contentment is great gain. *We brought nothing into this world, and we can take nothing out of it.* For the love of money is a root of all kinds of evil."

There are people who like to dispute the word of God. We all are on a quest for knowledge to learn about our Lord and Savior, Jesus Christ. We should seek after the things of God and not financial wealth. If you love money, you can't love God. God says, the love of money is a root of all kinds of evil.

DAY 253:
(September 11)

*Luke 4:1-4

"Then Jesus, being filled with the Holy Spirit, returned from the Jordan and was led by the Spirit into the wilderness. He was tempted forty days by the devil . . . He ate nothing . . . He was hungry. And the devil said, 'If You are the Son of God, command this stone to become bread.' *But Jesus said, 'Man shall not live by bread alone, but by every Word of God.'"*

Just as we need food to feed our nature bodies; we need Spiritual food to feed our Souls. The devil will always seek after the flesh to cause us to sin. God has put His word on the earth to feed the soul, to protect it against the tricks of the devil. Let's continue to read the Bible, God's word, to keep our spirits fed and protected against sin.

DAY 254:
(September 12)

Proverbs 6:7-9

"*When a man's ways please the Lord, He makes even his enemies to be at peace with him . . . A man's heart plans his way, but the Lord directs his steps.*"

When we put all our hearts, minds, and trust in the Lord, He will protect us from all hurt, harm, and danger. God will not let any harm come to His children. We decide what we want out of life, but the Lord orders our footsteps.

1 Thessalonians 5:16-24

"*Rejoice always, pray continually, and give thanks in all circumstances; for this is God's will for you in Christ Jesus.* Do not quench the Spirit . . . May your whole spirit, soul and body be kept blameless at the coming of the Lord Jesus Christ. The One who calls you is faithful, and will do it."

Let's keep our minds, bodies, and souls stayed on Jesus. We must always be thankful for what we have and what we are going through. If and when things get hard, *pray!* God will be and is always near. He wants to help us, but we must believe. Let's concentrate on following the Ten Commandments.

DAY 256:
(September 14)

1 John 3:14-18

"We know we have passed from death to life, because we love the brethren. He who does not love his brother abides in death . . . By this we know love, because He laid down His life for us. And we also ought to lay down our lives for the brethren. *But whoever has this world's goods, and sees his brother in need, and shuts up his heart . . . how does the love of God live in him?*"

We know we are a child of God when we begin to care about one another. God sent His Son Jesus to the earth to lay down His life for us. We are supposed to desire to be like Jesus. God wants us to be our brothers' keepers. Let's pray that we begin to do unto others as we would have them do unto us.

DAY 257:
(September 15)

*Colossians 3:1-10

"Since, then, you have been raised with Christ, set your hearts on things above, where Christ is . . . not on earthy things . . . *But now you must rid yourselves of all such things as these: anger, rage, malice, slander, and filthy language from your lips* . . . Do not lie to each other . . . and put on the new self . . ."

Since we are children of God, we should represent ourselves as such. A Christian should not go around using foul language, lying, and doing things against God. Let's respect each other in every way.

DAY 258:
(September 16)

Hebrews 4:9-13

There, then, remains a Sabbath-rest for the people of God; just as God did from His . . . For the word of God is alive and active. Sharper than any double-edged sword, it penetrates . . . *Nothing in creation is hidden from God's sight. Everything is uncovered and lay bare before the eyes of Him whom we must give an account."*

We must understand that we are going to die. But, we have a promise that if we live according to the word of God (The Bible), we have an eternal life. Let's pay attention to how we are living in this world. Let's do the will of God by loving each other.

DAY 259:
(September 17)

Genesis 1:1-5

In the beginning God created the heavens and the earth. The earth was without form, and void; and darkness was on the face of the deep . . . *Then God said, "Let there be light"; and there was light . . .*

God is the Creator of the world, universe and *all*. For this reason we call God the Author and the Finisher of our faith, the Alpha and the Omega, the Beginning and the End, and the First and the Last. Everything in this world is or came to be through our Lord and Savior, Jesus Christ.

DAY 260:
(September 18)

Matthew 18:18-20

"Assuredly, I say to you, whatever you bind on earth will be bound in heaven, and whatever you loose on earth will be loosed in heaven . . . *For where two or three are gathered together in My name, I am there in the midst of them.*"

We have power in God when we pray and ask for things in His name. It must be the will of God and be done with sincerity. God knows our hearts and wants us to ask for our requests from Him. When we pray, let's bring forth the Holy Spirit.

DAY 261:
(September 19)

1 Corinthians 13:1-7

"And yet I will show you the most excellent way . . . If I give all I possess to the poor and give over my body to hardship that I may boast, but do not have love, I gain nothing. *Love is patient, love is kind . . . it does not boast. It is not proud . . . it is self-seeking, it is not easily angered . . . It always protects trusts and hopes . . ."*

God is love. The Bible says love never fails; therefore God never fails. We can show how much we love by demonstrating God's definition of love. The light and love of God will shine through those who truly love.

DAY 262:
(September 20)

*Luke 5:31-32

"Jesus answered them, 'It is not the healthy who need a doctor, but the sick. *I have not come to call the righteous, but sinners to repentance.*"

Jesus makes the example clear to the disciples: "I have come to bring the sinners to repentance." Many people profess to be followers of Jesus, but we must remember that we all are sinners. God wants us to repent first, before we can move forward in Him.

DAY 263:
(September 21)

Isaiah 55:8-11

For My thoughts are not your thoughts, neither are your ways My ways, Declares the Lord . . . so My Word that goes out from My mouth: It will not return to me empty, but will accomplish what I desire and achieve the purpose for which I sent it."

The word is God and God is the word. Whatever is spoken in the Bible is God's own word. Whatever He says it is and whatever he spoke will come to pass. We are to stand firm on the word of God and have the faith to believe in whatever it says.

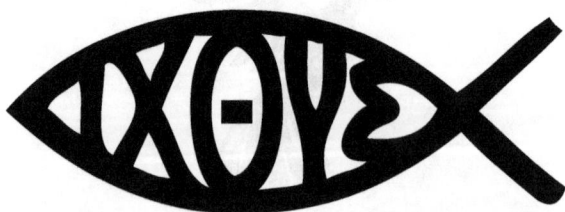

DAY 264:
(September 22)

1 Timothy 5:6-8

"Give the people these instructions, so that no one may be opened to blame. *Anyone who does not provide for their relatives, and especially for their own household, has denied the faith and is worse than an unbeliever.*"

We are to be our brother's keeper. How can we call ourselves a Christian, and not even take care of our fellow man? God says we are to provide for our relatives and especially our family members. Let's pray for a giving heart.

Prayer:

Lord, Jesus, I have preached my first sermon before Your people. Please continue to have Your way in my life. Use me for Your glory. Let the people hear what You have to say. I will ask that You let me decrease, while You increase. Let someone be saved, delivered, set free, or healed. I will continue to give You all the praise. I say this prayer, in Jesus' name, Amen.

DAY 265:
(September 23)

Psalm 91:1-7

"*He who dwells in the secret place of the Most High shall abide under the shadow of the Almighty* . . . He is my refuge and my fortress; my God, in Him I trust . . . A thousand may fall at your side, and ten thousand at your right hand; but it shall not come near you."

We should commune, rest, abide, stay close to God, and do as He expects from us. If we do these things, God will be a resting place for us when things are too hard to handle. He will cover, protect, and comfort us.

(September 24)

1 Corinthians 3:16-17

"*Don't you know that you yourselves are God's temple and that God's Spirit dwells in your midst?* If anyone destroys God's temple, God will destroy that person; for God's temple is sacred, and you together are the temple."

We are made in the image of God. God dwells within our hearts; therefore we need to acknowledge that fact. What we do to our bodies, we do to God. We should think twice before we do anything to hurt our bodies.

DAY 267:
(September 25)

Matthew 6:19-34

"Do not store up for yourselves treasures on earth . . . But store up treasures in heaven . . . do not worry about your life . . . Do not worry about clothes . . . But seek His kingdom and His righteousness, and these things will be given to you as well . . . *Therefore don't not worry about tomorrow, for tomorrow will worry about itself.*"

We are to depend on God for everything. We have no need to store up things and worry about this and that. God will supply *all* of our needs. He is Jehovah-Jireh, the Lord our Provider! He will see that all our needs are met.

DAY 268:
(September 26)

Romans 12:1-2

"Therefore, I urge you, brothers and sisters, in view of God's mercy, to offer your bodies as a living sacrifice, holy and pleasing to God . . . *Do not conform to the pattern of this world, but be transformed by the renewing of your mind . . .*"

We are to be representative of Jesus Christ. Everything we do should show God's love towards others. Every day we are to teach ourselves how to live holy unto God. God is holy and expects us to be the same. Let's pray for God to renew our minds to be more like Him.

Hebrews 11:1-7

"Now faith is confidence in what we hope for and assurance about what we do not see . . . *And without faith it is impossible to please God, because anyone who comes to Him must believe that He exists* and He rewards those who earnestly seek Him."

As believers, we must put our trust in the things we cannot see. Faith is trust. We have to believe in the promises of God and stand on His word. Along with the faith, we must also produce works because faith without works is dead. Then, God will bless (reward) us.

DAY 270:
(September 28)

1 Thessalonians 5:12-15

"Now we ask you . . . to acknowledge those who work hard among you . . . Hold them in the highest regard in love because of their work. *Live in peace with each other . . . Encourage the disheartened, help the weak, be patient with everyone.* Make sure that nobody pays back wrong for wrong."

We are to love one another as God loves us. We should help each other whenever the opportunity arises. Always look for an opportunity to lend a helping hand to a fellow man. Remember that two wrongs don't make a right. God is watching our every move.

DAY 271:
(September 29)

1 Peter 4:12-19

"Dear friend, do not be surprised at the fiery ordeal that has come to test you, as though something strange were happening to you. But rejoice inasmuch as you participate in the suffering of Christ . . . *However, if you suffer as a Christian, do not be ashamed, but praise God that you bear that name . . .*"

Jesus suffered on the cross for our sins. The Bible says that we may also suffer, but that does not mean it's a bad thing. God loves us so much; He gave His only begotten Son to die for us. Therefore, if He suffered, let us count it a joy to be a part of the kingdom.

DAY 272:
(September 30)

Revelation 3:1-6

"These are the words of Him who holds the seven spirits of God . . . I know your deeds . . . wake up! . . . what you have received and heard; hold fast, and repent. But if you do not wake up, I will come like a thief, and you will not know at what time I will come to you . . . *The one who is victorious will . . . be dressed in white. I will never blot out the name of that person from the Book of Life.*"

God is telling us to get ready and be ready upon His return. No man knows the day or hour He will come. It will be as quick as a thief in the night. If we do all we are commanded to do, we will surely be written in the Lamb's Book of Life. That should be our prayer: "Lord keep us in Your will. Help us to obey *Your* commandments."

Matthew 6:1-4

Be careful not to practice your righteousness in front of others to be seen by them. If you do, you will have no reward from your Father in heaven. So when you give to the needy, do not announce it . . . but when you give to the needy, do not let your right hand know what your left hand is doing."

We do not need to show off how righteous we are. We don't need to prove that we are righteous just to get approval from others. God sees and knows everything. He knew us before we were born, and He knows our every thought and action today. Do whatever you do as if you are doing it for God. He will be the one who will reward you for your righteousness.

ΩA

DAY 274:
(October 2)

2 Corinthians 5:11-15

"Since, then, we know what it is to fear the Lord, we try to persuade others. What we are is plain to God . . . For Christ's love compels us . . . *And He died for all, that those who live should no longer live for themselves but for Him who died for them and was raised again.*"

God knew us before the foundation of the world. He made us and predestined us for His purpose. God wants us to live our lives for His will and purpose. We should appreciate God for sending His Son, Jesus, to die for our sins.

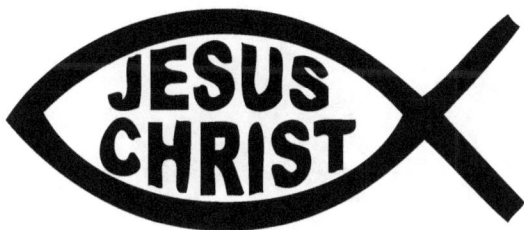

DAY 275:
(October 3)

John 10:7-11

"Therefore Jesus said again, 'Very truly I tell you, I am the gate for the sheep. All those who come before Me are thieves and robbers, but the sheep have not listened to them . . . whoever enters through Me will be saved . . . *The thief comes only to steal and kill and destroy; I come that they may have life, and have it to the full.*"

Satan is the thief. He is the one who comes to destroy God's sheep (His chosen people). Whoever will follow Jesus will be saved from evil. We must enter the gate of God and resist the tricks of the enemy. Satan is out to win as many souls as he can. Don't get caught in his tricks and snares.

DAY 276:
(October 4)

James 3:12-17

"My brothers and sisters, can a fig tree bear olives, or a grapevine bear figs? Neither can a salt spring produce fresh water . . . *For where you have envy and selfish ambition, there you find disorder and every evil practice* . . . Peacemakers who sow peace reap a harvest of righteousness."

You cannot serve two masters. You cannot worship God and the devil at the same time. Bitterness and self-seeking ambition are from the devil. God wants us to practice righteousness.

DAY 277:
(October 5)

*Luke 17:1-4

"Jesus said to His disciples: 'Things that cause people to stumble are bound to come, but woe to anyone through whom they come ... So watch your selves ...'"

Jesus tells His disciples that they are bound to fall into the temptations of the world, but they should hold fast to God. Jesus is the truth, the way, and the life. He mentions that no man can get to the Father, except through Him. Let's continue to be prayerful and watchful in everything we say and do.

DAY 278:
(October 6)

Hebrews 4:13-16

"Nothing in all creation is hidden from God's sight. Everything is uncovered and laid bare before the eyes of Him to whom we must give an account . . . *Let us then approach God's throne of grace with confidence, so that we may receive mercy and find grace to help us in time of need.*"

As we travel through this thing called life, we should try to live for Jesus. He is the gateway to our Father God. God sees and knows everything going on above and under the earth. At the end of this life, we must give an account of how we lived to please God. Let's pray that we live according to God's will and purpose for our lives.

Prayer:

God, I just want to thank You this morning for the many blessings You have bestowed upon me throughout this spiritual journey. I pray that You will continue to order my footsteps so I send out only what You want Your people to receive. I will continue to trust and love You in all that I do. I say this prayer in Jesus' name, Amen!

DAY 279:
(October 7)

*Proverbs 21:1-4

"In the Lord's hand the king's heart is a stream of water that channels toward all who please him. *A person may think their own ways are right, but the Lord weighs the heart . . .*"

God wants us to be true to the faith. He is watching to see who has true faith. When Jesus returns, He will be looking to see who has faith. As we go about our daily task, let's remember that God is watching us. He knows the underlying motives of everyone.

DAY 280:
(October 8)

*Isaiah 55:6-11

"Seek the Lord while He can be found; call on Him while He is near . . . *For My thoughts are not your thoughts, neither your ways my ways, declares the Lord . . .*"

Today is the day to accept Jesus Christ as your Lord and Savior. He is always near and waiting to receive you into the kingdom. God's ways are not like our ways, and His thoughts are not like our thoughts. Whatever He speaks, He makes come to pass.

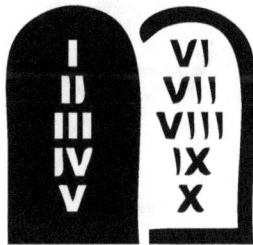

DAY 281:
(October 9)

Philippians 4:19-20

"*And my God will meet all your needs according to the riches of His glory in Christ Jesus.* To our God and Father be glory for ever and ever. Amen."

Our God is the Creator of everything. Everything in and on the earth is the Lord's. He is rich in more than material things. God says, ask and you shall receive. Draw near to God, and He will draw near to you.

DAY 282:
(October 10)

*Psalm 19:14

"*Let the words of my mouth and the meditation of my heart be acceptable in Your sight*, O Lord, my strength and my Redeemer.

Our prayer today must be to be pleasing in God's sight. He wants us to be true to Him and serve Him with all of our hearts, minds, souls, and might. He is our strength and help in times of need.

DAY 283:
(October 11)

*1 John 5:1-5

Whoever believes that Jesus is the Christ is born of God . . .
For this is the love of God, that we keep His commandments.
And His commandments are not burdensome . . ."

We must first believe that Jesus is the son of God. Then, we
must keep His commandments because God made them
easy to follow. God says if His commandments are hard for
you to keep, then the love of Christ is not in you.

DAY 284:
(October 12)

Romans 14:11-14

"For it is written . . . 'every knee shall bow to Me, and every tongue shall confess to God.' So then each of us shall give an account of himself to God. *Therefore let us not judge one another anymore . . . not put a stumbling block or a cause to fall in our brother's way.*"

When it's all said and done and we are at the end of time, everyone will bow down to God and serve Him. We must give an account to God for whatever we do in this life at the judgment. Let's do everything according to His will and purpose, so He will be pleased. We are our brothers' keepers.

Matthew 7:9-14

"What man is there among you who, if his son asks for bread, will give him a stone? Or if he asks for fish, will give him a serpent . . . *Therefore, whatever you want men to do to you, do also to them, for this is the Law . . .*"

Do unto to others, as you would have them do unto you. Treat others like you want to be treated. God sees everything we do. Better than that, He knows the motives behind what you are doing. Let's pray to have god-like love towards everyone. Let's love people like God loves us.

DAY 286:
(October 14)

Psalm 62:5-8

"Yes my soul, find rest in God; my hope comes from Him. Truly He is my Rock and my Salvation . . . *Trust in Him at all times, you people; pour out your hearts to Him, for God is our refuge.*"

God is our source of peace. He will comfort us when we are low. We ought to always seek the Lord when we feel depressed. The Lord is our Shepherd. Trusting in God is the key to our relationship with Him.

2 Corinthians 13:11-14

"Finally, brothers and sisters, rejoice! *Strive for full restoration, encourage one another, be of one mind, live in peace. And the God of love and peace will be with you.* Greet one another with a holy kiss . . ."

God wants us to live in harmony with one another. We should always strive to care for and protect one another. We are our brothers' keepers. God wants us to teach one another the things we know about Him. He wants us on one accord in the faith.

DAY 288:
(October 16)

James 4:12-17

"There is only One Lawgiver and Judge, the One who is able to save and destroy. *But you—who are you to judge your neighbor? If anyone, then, knows the good they ought to do and doesn't do it, it is sin.*"

God Almighty, is the one and only judge of man. We should stop worrying about how everyone else is living and begin to concentrate on our own relationship with God.

DAY 289:
(October 17)

Mark 10:23-27

"Jesus looked around and said to His disciples, 'How hard it is for the rich to enter the kingdom of God?' His disciples were amazed . . . Jesus said . . . *It is easier for a camel to go through the eye of a needle than for someone who is rich to enter the kingdom of God . . .*"

All things are possible for those who love and trust God. We are not to rely on material things, such as money, homes, cars, jewelry, and so forth. These things are temporal. God is offering us eternal life in the place of our worldly possessions.

DAY 290:
(October 18)

Colossians 3:12-17

"Therefore, as the elect of God, holy, and beloved, put on tender mercies, kindness, humility, meekness, longsuffering; bearing with one another . . . But above all these things put on love . . . *And let the peace of God rule in your hearts, to which also you were called in one body; and be thankful . . ."*

We are all chosen and called by God to work for His kingdom. We must put away the things of the world and strive for holiness. Love is the key to forming a personal relationship with our Father God. God will give us the peace and understanding we need to minister to God's people.

DAY 291:
(October 19)

Luke 9:23-27

Then He said to them all, 'If anyone desires to come after Me, let him deny himself and take up his cross daily, and follow Me. For whoever desires to save his life will lose it, but whoever loses his life for My sake will save it. *For what profit is it to a man if he gains the whole world, and is himself destroyed or lost?"*

If we are to get closer to God, we must deny ourselves and follow Him with our whole heart. To be saved is to lose the life we are living. We must put away all of the things that connect us to this world, for example, strife, envy, malice, greed, fornication, and so on.

DAY 292:
(October 20)

Romans 15:4-7

"For everything that was written in the past was written to teach us . . . May the God who gives endurance and encouragement give you the same attitude of mind towards one another that Christ had. *Accept one another, then, just as Christ accepted you, in order to bring praise to God.*"

All the words of the Bible are there to teach us how to live for God. We are to embrace these scriptures and learn how to become Christ-like, spiritual and holy. Love is the key to living for God, because God is love.

DAY 293:
(October 21)

Titus 2:6-8

"*Encourage the young men to be self-controlled. In everything set an example by doing what is good.* In your teaching *show integrity, seriousness* and soundness of speech that cannot be condemned . . ."

We as mature children of God should teach the younger generation the ways of life. We are to be an example of how to love: God first, and then one another. We should always be ready to teach our children about the love of God and how to follow Him.

DAY 294:
(October 22)

**Romans 12:9-13

"Love must be sincere. Hate whatever is evil; cling to what is good. Be devoted to one another in love. *Honor one another above yourselves.* Never be lack in zeal . . . Practice hospitality."

We must be serious about our walk and relationship with God. Always hold on and strive to increase or improve your relationship with God. Love one another with god-like love. Let your love be genuine.

DAY 295:
(October 23)

*3 John 2-4

"*I pray that you may enjoy good health and that all may be well with you, even as your soul is getting along well* . . . I have no greater joy than to hear that my children are walking in the truth."

The message has come to God's people that we should be successful and strive to be the best we can be. It is our destiny and God's will that we be in good health as we prosper through this life. Let's walk according to God's will and accept His word as the truth.

DAY 296:
(October 24)

Isaiah 55:11-12

"*So is My word that goes out of My mouth: It will not return to Me empty, but will accomplish what I desire and achieve the purpose for which I sent it.* You will go out in peace . . ."

God's word is the truth and life. God is the word and the word is God. There are many promises within the Bible. He is letting us know that He will fulfill those promises. He wants us to have peace, joy, and happiness. His will is for us to prosper, be in good health, and live in love.

*Psalm 37:21-26

"The wicked borrows and does not repay, but the righteous shows mercy and gives . . . *The steps of a good man are ordered by the Lord, and He delights in his way* . . . I have been young, and now am old; yet I have not seen the righteous forsaken, nor his descendants begging bread."

God delights in someone who lives according to His will and His way. He will order your footsteps towards righteousness. He takes pleasure in seeing His children doing well. It is His will that we all be blessed. We are His masterpiece. He will bless us and our children.

DAY 297:
(October 26)

*Deuteronomy 6:4-9

"The Lord our God, the Lord is one! *You shall love the Lord your God with all your heart, with all your soul, and with all your strength* . . . These words shall be in your heart . . . teach them to your children . . ."

God has commanded us to show our love towards Him by putting our hearts into loving Him. We should put the love of God deep down in our souls, minds, and spirits. We should put God in our heart, as God is in us. Let our children tell their children, and so forth and so on.

DAY 298:
(October 27)

*__Matthew 10:37-39__

"He who loves father or mother more than Me is not worthy of Me . . . And whoever does not take up his cross and follow after Me is not worthy of Me. *He who finds his life will lose it, and whoever loses his life for My sake will find it*"

We serve a jealous God. He wants us to put all of our hearts into loving Him and Him alone. Mothers and fathers will leave us, one day, even if it is through death. But, the Lord will be with us even after death. Once we commit to God, we enter into a new life. Our life is with God and in God.

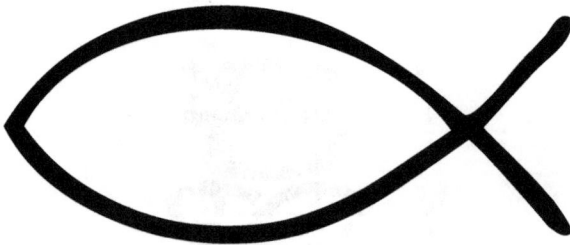

DAY 299:
(October 28)

Psalm 121:1-8

"*I will lift up my eyes to the hill—from whence comes my help? My help comes from the Lord, who made heaven and earth. He will not allow your foot to be moved; He who keeps you will not slumber . . .*"

Although trials and storms may come; we can look towards the hills, from where our help comes. God, who is in heaven, is where our help comes from. He will protect us from all hurt, harm, and danger. He has eyes in every place, and He never sleeps. He is always waiting, ready, and available to answer our prayers.

Prayer:

Father, I just want to pray today for everyone who has experienced any misfortunes of any kind. Storms may come, but God is in control of everything. You made the winds and the rain. We will trust You, even when we cannot see the end of the matter. Send protecting angels to guard our loved ones through our messy time. We give You honor and praise, Amen.

DAY 300:
(October 29)

*Proverbs 3:3-7

"Let not mercy and trust forsake you; bind them around your neck . . . *Trust in the Lord with all your heart, and lean not to your own understanding; In all your ways acknowledge Him, and He will direct your path . . .*"

Whatever we learn from the scriptures, keep them close to your heart. There are many promises in the Bible; therefore, learn them to carry you through the hard times. God's ways are not like our ways. His thoughts are not like our thoughts. If we let go and let God control our lives, He will give us peace and joy.

DAY 301:
(October 30)

*2 Corinthians 1:3-7

"*Praise be to God* . . . the Father of compassion and God of all comfort, *who comforts us in all our troubles, so that we can comfort those in any trouble with the comfort we ourselves receive from God* . . . And our hope for You is firm . . ."

God is our God of comfort. Whenever we feel a need to be comforted, God wants us to depend on Him. He is always available and ready to comfort us. Once we know and understand the love of God; we can share the Good News with others. God wants us to use our brokenness to minister to those who are hurting.

DAY 302:
(October 31)

*1 Corinthians 10:12-15

"Therefore let him who thinks he stands take heed lest he fall. No temptation has overtaken you except such as is common to man; but *God is faithful, who will not allow you to be tempted beyond what you may be able to bear it . . .*"

We will all be tempted at one time or another, in our lifetimes. Remember, God knows all about it. He will always come in to help if you ask Him. So, whenever you feel or think you are sinning against God, pray for Him to send you strength to overcome it.

(November 1)

*Luke 6:46-49

"Why do you call Me, 'Lord, Lord,' and do not do what I say? As for everyone who comes to Me and hears My words and puts them into practice, I will show you what they are like . . . *But the one who hears My word and does not put them into practice is* like *a man who built a house on the ground without a foundation . . .*"

God wants us to be doers of the word. The word is God and God is the word and God is love. We are to put the word in our hearts and share them with others. God wants us to love our neighbors and share His good news as we love one another.

John 6:61-65

"When Jesus knew in Himself that His disciples complained about this, He said to them, 'Does this offend you . . .?'*It is the Spirit who gives life; the flesh profits nothing. The words that I speak to you are Spirit, and they are life . . .*"

Every word in the Bible is directly from God, the Father. God is the word and the word is God. God said His word became flesh (Jesus) and dwelt among the people. Every word that comes from God is from His Holy Spirit, and it will bring Life. It will bring us life with Jesus Christ.

DAY 305:
(November 3)

*Revelation 22:7-14

"Behold, I am coming quickly! Blessed is he who keeps the words of the prophecy of this book ... And He said to me, Do not seal the words of the prophecy of this book, for the time is at hand ... *I am the Alpha and the Omega, the Beginning and the End, the First and the Last. Blessed are those who do His commandments.* "

We are living in the end of time. The world is coming to an end, and Jesus will return. We are to be alert and sober, ready to be with the Lord. He is the Alpha (We should put Him first in our lives), He is the Omega (We should make Him the last thing on our minds when we retire for the day), (We should make God the first thing on our minds, when we wake up), and He is the Beginning and the End (The beginning and the end of our everything). God was the One and only one on this earth, before there was anything or anybody. He created *all* things and *all* people, animals and creeping things. Let's put our lives in order to be accepted by our Father and Lord Jesus Christ.

DAY 306:
(November 4)

Lamentations 3:21-26

"This I recall to my mind, therefore I have hope. *Through the Lord's mercies we are not consumed, because His compassions fail not.* They are new every morning . . . The Lord is good to those who wait for Him, to the soul who seeks Him."

We must put all of our hope and trust in the Lord. He loves us so much, He died for us. As many times as we fail God's instructions for us, He will always forgive us. He wants us to continue to seek after Him and His righteousness. It takes patience and prayer to stay connected to God.

DAY 307:
(November 5)

1 Kings 8:56-61

Praise be to the Lord who has given rest to His people Israel just as He promised. Not one word has failed . . . *May He turn our hearts to Him, to walk in obedience to Him and keep His commands . . . He gave our ancestors . . ."*

This is our prayer today. We want to be fully committed to God. We want to turn our entire life over to Him who is the giver of life. We want to live in Him and for Him to live in us. Our prayer today is to dedicate our hearts, minds, and souls to serving (following) God. Let's ask God to create in us a clean heart and renew a right spirit in us. We will serve Him from this day forward.

*Mark 11:20-26

"In the morning, as they went along, they saw a fig tree withered from the roots. Peter said to Jesus, 'Rabbi, look!' The fig tree You cursed has withered! 'Have faith in God', Jesus answered . . . whatever you ask for in prayer, believe that you have received it, and it will be yours. *And when you stand praying, if you hold anything against anyone, forgive them, so that your Father in heaven may forgive your sins.'"*

Jesus cursed a fig tree while walking with Peter. Peter was amazed, but Jesus reminded him to "Have faith in God! ' Jesus wants us to know that we can have whatever we ask for from God if we ask in faith. We must believe in God and believe we will receive what we ask for. Let's put all our trust in the Lord.

DAY 309:
(November 7)

1 John 2:15-17

"Do not love the world or anything in the world. If anyone loves the world, the love of the Father is not in them . . . *The world and its desires pass away, but whoever does the will of God lives forever.*"

The world is full of sin, lust, and pride, which are evil in the eyes of God. He wants us to rid our spirits, hearts, and minds of loving these things. God wants us to follow His commandments and spread the good news to the entire world.

DAY 310:
(November 8)

1 Chronicles 28:9

'As for you, my son Solomon, know the God of your father, and *serve Him with a loyal heart and a willing mind; for the Lord searches all hearts and understands all the intent of the thoughts.* If you seek Him, He will be found by you; but if you forsake Him, He will cast you off forever."

Trust your Lord God with your whole heart, mind, body, and soul. We need to not only just talk the talk but also walk the walk. God is paying attention to those who say they love Him. Let's seek after God so that He can allow everything else to follow.

(November 9)

1 Corinthians 3:16-17

"*Do you not know that you are the temple of God and that the Spirit of God dwells in you?* If anyone defiles the temple of God, God will destroy him. For the temple of God is holy, which temple are you."

We are made in the image of God. We should present our bodies, as living sacrifices, back to God. What we put in our bodies, and what we do to our bodies, is a reflection of what and how we feel about our Lord. Let's begin to understand how sacred, special, and important our bodies are. We belong to God. We live in God, and God dwells in us.

1 John 4:7-16

"Beloved, let us love one another, for love is of God . . . He who does not love does not know God, for God is love . . . *Whoever confesses that Jesus is the Son of God, God abides in him, and he in God."*

God is love. We are one with God when we love one another. God wants us to love each other, just as He loves us. If we say we love God and do not love one another; we are lying to ourselves and God. Let's show god-like love toward one another.

DAY 313:
(November 11)

Joshua 1:7-9

Be strong and very courageous. Be careful to obey all the law my servant Moses gave to you; do not turn from it to the right or to the left . . . *Be strong and courageous. Do not be afraid; do not be discouraged, for the Lord your God will be with you wherever you go."*

God wants us to remember to follow the commandments He gave to us through Moses. We are to obey them the same as our ancestors. If we follow God's instructions, we will prosper and be in good health. God promised us He will never leave us or forsake us.

Prayer for Veterans:

Lord I come to You this day, to thank You for protecting our men and women who risk their lives for the United States of America. Continue to dispatch angels around the war zones and bring our soldiers home safely to their families. God, we will continue to honor You above everything and everyone. We Thank You, Jesus; Thank You, Jesus.

DAY 314:
(November 12)

Proverbs 4:18-27

"The path of the righteous is like the morning sun . . . But the way of the wicked is like deep darkness . . . Pay attention to what I say; turn your ear to My words . . . *Above all else, guard your heart, for everything you do flows from it . . . Do not turn to the right or to the left; keep your foot from evil.*"

God has given us a choice in life. We can walk in the light that is in Him, or walk in the darkness which is of the devil. God has laid out how we should please Him. It is up to us to love and obey Him or continue to disobey Him. He wants us to have everlasting life.

DAY 315:
(November 13)

Romans 3:18-27

"There is no fear of God before their eyes . . . Therefore no one will be declared righteous in God's sight by the works of the law; rather, through the law we become conscious of our sin . . . This righteousness is given through faith in Jesus Christ . . . *for all have sinned and fallen short of the glory of God . . ."*

We must put our faith into action. God will not just look at how well we carry out His works, but how true our faith is in Him. No one will be considered righteous, except the ones with true faith. This all comes to us through the grace of God.

DAY 316:
(November 14)

*Matthew 7:1-5

"*Judge not, that you be not judged. For what judgment you judge, you will be judged;* and with the measure you use, it will be measured back to you . . ."

We need to first look at our own lives before trying to judge others. By judging someone, we put the judgment back onto ourselves. How we judge someone is how we will be judged during the judgment of Christ.

DAY 317:
(November 15)

1 Peter 4:7-11

"But the end of all things is at hand; therefore be serious and watchful in your prayers. And above all things have fervent love for one another, for 'love will cover a multitude of sins' . . . *As each one has received a gift, minister it to one another, as good stewards . . .*"

As mentioned many times, we are living in the end of time. God is letting us know that it is time to get serious about our relationship with Him. He has commissioned us to preach the gospel and spread the word throughout the world. Our responsibility to God is to be fishermen of men.

Jeremiah 17:5-10

"Cursed is the man who trusts in man and makes flesh his strength, whose heart departs from the Lord . . .,*Blessed is the man who trusts in the Lord, and whose hope is the Lord . . . The Lord searches the heart . . .*"

God promises to bless us with all of our needs. We just have to trust Him in everything we do. We must put our lives into the Lord's hands and lean not to our own understanding. God is the author and finisher of our faith. Trust and faith are the keys to our blessings.

DAY 319:
(November 17)

Ecclesiastes 3:1-8

"*To everything there is a season, a time for every purpose under the heaven: A time to be born . . . A time to kill . . . A time to weep . . . A time to gain . . . A time to tear . . . A time to love and a time to hate.*"

We must remember that everything and everybody belongs to God. We were created for His purpose. Whatever we are going through is because of His power and according to His will. Our prayer should always be, "Lord let Your will be done." We all have seasons in our lives.

Prayer:

Lord, forgive me for falling behind in my morning inspirations. I'm praying that You will continue to lead and guide me along this journey. Help me Lord to keep on track and not fall off task. I trust and believe that all things work together for our good. I want to thank You, Lord, for increasing the people receiving the morning inspirations. It is only because of Your grace that these messages continue to flourish. Keep protecting me and my family and watch over us as we continue to do Your will. Amen!

DAY 320:
(November 18)

James 3:1-6

"*Where do wars and fights come from among you? Do they not come from your desires for pleasure that war in your members? You lust and do not have . . . You ask and do not receive because you ask in amiss . . .*"

All of our fights and quarrels come from within us. We are fighting a lust demon that dwells inside of us. Some of us pray and ask God for those things of the world that God is against. He wants us to pray for things that will connect us to Him.

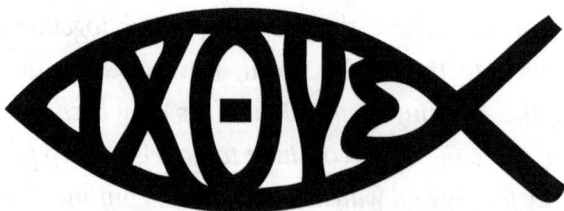

DAY 321:
(November 19)

Hebrews 13:15-16

"Therefore by Him let us continually offer the sacrifice of praise to God, that is, the fruit of our lips, giving thanks to His name. *But do not forget to do good* and *to share, for with such sacrifices God is pleased.*"

Our praise to God is the fruit of our lips. God wants us to continually give Him praise. It is our praise that connects us to God. Sometimes we may feel down, but that is when we give a sacrifice of praise—and that is when God will lift us up.

DAY 322:
(November 20)

Proverbs 29:22-26

"An angry man stirs up strife, and a furious man abounds in transgression. *A man's pride will bring him low, but the humble in spirit will retain honor.*"

We have a choice to have pride or to be humble. God wants us to put away our prideful attitudes and become humble. A humble man will have honor in the eyes of God. Let's pray for a humble heart and love one another as Christ loves us.

DAY 323:
(November 21)

*Leviticus 19:11-19

"You shall not steal, nor deal falsely, nor lie to one another. You shall not swear by My name falsely . . . you shall not cheat your neighbor . . . you shall not hate your brother in your heart . . . *you shall not take vengeance, nor bear any grudge against . . . your people, but you shall love your neighbor as yourself*: I am the Lord."

God lays out the commandments for us to follow. These commandments help us to stay closer to our Lord and Savior, Jesus Christ. Our Number 1 commandment is to love our neighbor as ourselves. Love is God and to love is godly.

DAY 324:
(November 22)

God Bless Everyone Who Reads This Book!

*Romans 8:24-28

"For we were saved in this hope, but hope that is seen is not hope; for why does one still hope for what he sees? But if we hope for what we do not see, we eagerly wait for it with perseverance . . . *And we know that all things work together for good to those who love God . . .*"

The Bible says, faith is the substance of things hoped for and the evidence of things not seen. If we can see what we hope for; it is not of God. God wants us to depend on Him for our hope. As we travel through this life, we are to let go and let God have His way. The things we go through will work together for our good. Let God's will be done.

DAY 325:
(November 23)

Colossians 2:6-8

"*So then, just as you receive Christ Jesus as Lord, continue to live your lives in Him, rooted and built up in Him, strengthened in the faith as you were taught, and overflowing with thankfulness.* See that no one takes you captive through hollow and deceptive philosophy, which depends on human tradition and the elemental spiritual forces of the world rather than on Christ."

The devil; Satan, is the lying deceiver, dwelling in the earth to turn hearts towards himself *The devil is a fallen angel, who was cast out of heaven for trying to be better than God. He is a tricky, crafty evil spirit who wants us to turn away from God. Let's stay in constant prayer and ask God to protect us from Satan's negative forces.*

DAY 326:
(November 24)

1 John 14-18

"We know that we have passed from death to life, because we love each other. Anyone who does not love remains in death . . . This is how we know what love is: Christ laid down His life for us . . . *Let us not love with words or speech but with actions and in truth.*"

God sent His only begotten Son; to come into the world, and die for our sins. This was the ultimate show of true, genuine, Love. We must return that same kind of god-like love towards others. God is love, and love is God. The Bible says that love covers a multitude of sins.

DAY 327:
(November 25)

Matthew 7:1-5

"Do not judge anyone, or you too will be judged. For in the same way you judge others, you will be judged, and with the same measure you use, it will be measured to you . . . *Why do you look at the speck of sawdust in your brother's eye and pay no attention to the plank in your own eye? . . . First take the plank out of your eye, and then you will see clearly to remove the speck from your brother's eye.*"

We have a habit of trying to minister to others before looking at our own situations. God wants us to clean out our own house (temple), before attempting to help someone else. *Do not* judge another; remember, you will be judged.

DAY 328:
(November 26)

2 Timothy 2:11-13

"Here is a trustworthy saying: If we die with Him, we will live with Him; *if we endure, we will also reign with Him. If we disown Him, He will disown us . . ."*

We must die of our flesh and be born again in Jesus Christ. We must keep our faith until we are united with Him. We are required to tell others about the goodness of the Lord. If we do not recognize Jesus as our Lord and Savior, He will not recognize us as His children. We are all children of the living God.

DAY 329:
(November 27)

*Ephesians 3:13-20

"Therefore I ask that you do not lose heart at my tribulations for you, which is your glory . . . That He would grant you, according to the riches in glory . . . That Christ may dwell in your hearts through faith . . . *Now to Him who is able to do exceedingly, abundantly about all that we ask or think; according to the power that work in us.*"

Paul explains to us the love God has for us all. Because we are the seed of Abraham, we are given the promises of God's eternal love. God has given us inner power to understand His love. It is our will and strength in Jesus that will bring us closer to God.

DAY 330:
(November 28)

Galatians 4:8-10

"But then, indeed when you did not know God, you served those which by nature are not gods . . . *But now after you have known God, rather are known by God, how is it you turn again to the weak and beggarly elements, to which you desire again to be in bondage . . .*"

We are all children of God. Once we turn our lives to God and begin to serve Him with our whole heart, He wants us to *never* turn away again. He wants us to stay connected to Him. We need to always pray for increased faith. God will keep us close. Let's keep God on our minds.

DAY 331:
(November 29)

1 Thessalonians 4:14-23

"Now we exhort you, brethren, warn those who are unruly, *comfort the fainthearted, uphold the weak, be patient with all.* See that no one renders evil for evil to anyone, *but always pursue what is good* both for your selves and for all. *Rejoice always, pray without ceasing, in everything give thanks;* for this is the will of God . . ."

We are our brothers' keepers. When we see our fellow man doing things against God, we should be concerned. We should always do to others as we would have them do to us. Let's continue to pray for one another. God wants us all to enter the kingdom of heaven.

DAY 332:
(November 30)

Ecclesiastes 7:16-22

"*Do not be overly righteous, nor be overly wise . . . Also do not take to heart everything people say,* lest you hear your servant cursing you. For many times, also, your own heart has known that even you have cursed others."

God does not want us to be overly righteous, trying to be "holier than thou." Too much of anything is a disservice to God. He does not want us to think we are above another. We must always remember where we came from. We all have sinned and came short of God's glory.

DAY 333:
(December 1)

James 1:16-22

"Don't be deceived . . . Every good and perfect gift is from above, coming down from the Father . . . Take note of this: *Everyone should be quick to listen, slow to speak and slow to become angry,* because human anger does not produce the righteousness that God desires . . . Do not merely listen to the word . . . Do what it says."

God gives us everything we need in this life. He wants us to be still and know that He is God. He is the Creator of the universe. Let's be still and listen for Him to speak to us. Let's not get weary in well doing. Let's hold on to our faith and know God will see us through.

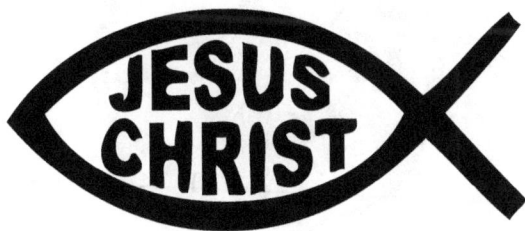

DAY 334:
(December 2)

Psalm 119:33-37

"Teach me, Lord, the way of Your decrees . . . *Give me understanding, so that I may keep Your law and obey it with all my heart* . . . Turn my heart towards Your statues and not towards selfish gain . . ."

Let's ask the Lord to lead and guide us toward the path of righteousness. We get all of our strength from the Lord. He tells us to serve and love Him with: "all of our heart, mind, soul, and strength." When we connect to God, it should be from the heart.

DAY 335:
(December 3)

*Hebrews 6:1-6

"*Therefore let us move beyond the elementary teachings about Christ and be taken forward to maturity,* nor laying again the foundation of repentance from acts that lead to death . . ."

God wants us to continue moving forward in Him . . . Do not be satisfied with just the basic knowledge and understanding of Christ. He wants us to seek after Him for ourselves by reading the Bible and staying on our faces, praying.

Philippians 4:8-13

"Finally . . . whatever things are true . . . noble . . . meditate on these things . . . The things which you learned and received and heard . . . these do and the God of peace will be with you . . . *I have learned in whatever state I am' to be content. I can do all things through Christ who strengthens me."*

God wants us to meditate day and night on His word. God is the word and the word is God. As we learn about the goodness of the Lord, we are to keep it hidden in our hearts. Our prayer should always be: "Let Your will be done!" God will supply all of our needs, according to the riches in His glory.

(December 5)

*2 Corinthians 13:5-9

"Examine yourselves to see whether you are in the faith; test yourselves . . . For we are glad when we are weak and you are strong. And this also we pray that you may be made complete."

Let's take a good look into our hearts to see where we stand with God. God looks at the heart; while man looks at the outward appearance. We need to test our faith and know that we are children of God.

ΩA

DAY 338:
(December 6)

Ecclesiastes 12:13-14

"Let us hear the conclusion of the whole matter: Fear God and keep His commandment, for this is man's all. *For God will bring into judgment, including every secret thing, whether good or evil.*"

God has His eyes on everything we do and say. He has given us the law (commandments) to live by. All He asks us to do is *do good, love one another, and tell others about His everlasting love, for God is love. When the judgment comes, we should expect to hear Him say:* "Well done, My good and faithful servant." *That should be our goal in life.*

DAY 339:
(December 7)

1 John 4:7-13

"Beloved, let us love one another, for love is of God: and everyone who loves is born of God and knows God is love . . . If God loved us, we also ought to love one another. *No one has seen God at any time. If we love one another, God abides in us, and His Love has been perfected in us.*"

God is love and to love is of God. God wants us to love one another. We know we have been made complete in God if we love one another—even our neighbors. God said for us to love our neighbors as ourselves. How can we call ourselves a child of God, and not love one another? We know we live in God when we love all God's people.

2 Peter 1:3-9

"His divine power has given us everything we need for a godly life through our knowledge of Him who called us by His own glory and goodness . . . *For this very reason, make every effort to add to your faith goodness; and to goodness, knowledge . . . self-control . . . perseverance . . . mutual affection and love . . .* Whoever does not have them is nearsighted and blind . . ."

When God sent His Holy Spirit to live in us, that was the beginning of our relationship with Him. From there, all we need to do is strengthen our faith. Faith in God is the key to a fulfilled life. Let's pray and ask God to increase our faith. He said, "faith without works is dead." Therefore, we must put our faith into action.

DAY 341:
(December 9)

Hebrews 11:1-3

"*Now faith is the substance of things hoped for, the evidence of things not seen . . .* By faith we understand that the worlds were formed by the word of God, so that the things which are seen were not made of things which are visible."

Faith is the one thing that pleases God. Without faith it is impossible to please God. We should always ask God to increase our faith. God wants us to activate our faith at all times. Faith without works is dead.

Philippians 4:4-7

"Rejoice in the Lord . . . Let your gentleness be evidence to all. The Lord is near. *Do not be anxious for anything, but in every situation, by prayer and petition, with thanksgiving, present your requests to God . . . And the peace of God . . . will guard your hearts and minds. . ."*

No matter what situation you are in, rejoice and give God praise. Nothing happens to us without God knowing about it. This is the golden opportunity to show God how much you love Him and trust Him. Never try to do anything without taking it to God in prayer.

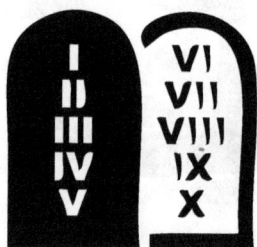

DAY 343:

(December 11)

2 Chronicles 7:11-16

"When Solomon had finished the temple . . . the Lord appeared to him at night . . . when I shut up the heavens so that there is no rain . . . *if My people, who are called by My name, will humble themselves and pray and seek My face and turn from their wicked ways, then I will hear from heaven, and I will forgive their sin and heal their land* . . . I have chosen and consecrated this temple so that My name may be there forever."

King Solomon, the son of David, built the temple of God as he was instructed. Once it was finished, the Lord appeared before him to let him know this would be His (God's) house of worship. God wants us to continue to worship and pray, and He will continue to be our God. He will forgive our sin and heal our land, just as He has promised.

DAY 344:
(December 12)

Luke 11:9-5-10

"Then Jesus said . . . suppose you have a friend . . . and you ask him to lend you three loaves of bread . . . and he said he has no bread . . . the door is already locked . . . because of friendship, he will surely get up and give you as much as you need . . . *Ask and it will be given to you, seek and you will find; knock and the door will be opened to you . . .*"

If we have a relationship with God; He is our friend. If we seek after Him, He will be found. If we knock, He will open the door for us. If we ask Him for anything, He will provide—as long as it's according to His will. We must look at God as our friend. He loves us that much.

DAY 345:
(December 13)

Matthew 5:3-12

"Blessed are the poor in spirit . . . Blessed are those who mourn . . . Blessed are the meek . . . Blessed are those who thirst after righteousness . . . Blessed are the pure in heart . . . *Blessed are you when people insult you, persecute you and falsely say all kinds of evil against you because of Me. Rejoice and be glad, because great is your reward in heaven . . .*"

Every one of us can be found in one or more of these positions where God will bless us. God says to just let these things roll off, because our reward is in heaven. Let's not allow the devil to cause us to sin because of being persecuted. These things are bound to happen, but keep looking toward our Father, who art in heaven.

Prayer:

Heavenly Father, I am coming toward the end of this assignment. I have made a commitment to write a morning inspirational manuscript for a period of 365 days. Lord, the people that are receiving these messages are requesting that I continue this assignment past the one year obligation. Help me, Lord. People are getting saved, healed, and set free. I want to thank you, God, for allowing me to minister to Your people, every morning. It is only because of You that this book is going to be a bestseller. I pray that people from all over the world will want to read this book and make this world a better place to live in. I give You all the glory, honor, and praise for giving me the strength and patience to complete this assignment. Father, let me know what is next for me to do for You. I only want to do Your will. I only want to please You, Lord, and not seek my own pleasures. My prayer today is: I want to know what You want me to do after this book is completed. Thank you, Lord, and I love You. I say this prayer and all my prayers, in Jesus' name, Amen!

DAY 346:
(December 14)

*Romans 15:14-22

"I myself am convinced . . . that you yourselves are full of goodness, filled with knowledge and competent to instruct one another . . . I have fully proclaimed the gospel of Christ. . .As it is written, *Those who were not told about Him will see, and those who have not heard will understand . . .*"

Paul, a servant of Christ Jesus, was sent to tell the people about his relationship with God. He wanted to let them know that he was a witness to Jesus' signs, wonders, and miracles. God wants us to know we too have that same power. We are to go out into the world and preach the gospel of Jesus Christ.

DAY 347:
(December 15)

2 Timothy 1:6-9

"Therefore I remind you to stir up the gift of God which is in you through the laying of hands. *For God has not given us a spirit of fear, but of power and of love and of a sound mind.* Therefore do not be ashamed of the testimony of our Lord . . ."

God has given us the power that was given to His Son, Jesus Christ. We are to use this power to heal, set free, and deliver others. We are to be bold in delivering the gospel of Jesus Christ and not be ashamed.

DAY 348:
(December 16)

I am thanking God for allowing me to see another day. . Today, I pray that this morning inspiration will touch the lives of God's people to help another person, and so on.

1 Thessalonians 4:9-12

"Now about your love for one another . . . for you yourselves have been taught by God to love each other . . . make it your ambition to lead a quiet life: *You should mind your own business and work with your hands . . . so that you will not be dependent on anybody.*"

God always tells us to love our neighbor, love one another, and love your enemy. God is love, and to love is being god-like. We should work because it says if a man does not work, he cannot eat. Let's ask God to help us with minding our own business and keep our minds on Him.

DAY 349:
(December 17)

Ecclesiastes 3:9-13

What do workers gain for their toil? I have seen the burden God has laid on the human race. He has made everything beautiful in its time . . . *I know that there is nothing better for people than to be happy and do good while they live . . ."*

Everything was made by God, and made for God. We are here for God's purpose. We have everything we need to survive, yet we are not satisfied. The necessities of life are a gift from God. God wants us to enjoy our lives on earth, be happy, and seek after Him.

DAY 350:
(December 18)

*John 3:16-21

"For God so loved the world that He gave His only begotten Son, that whoever believes in Him should not perish but have everlasting life. *For God did not send His Son into the world to condemn the world, but that the world through Him might be saved . . ."*

God loves us so much; that He offered His very own Son, to die for our sins. He said in His word, what greater love is it than for a man to lay down his life for his fellow man. He proved His love for us. God wants us to be Christ-like in everything we say and do.

DAY 351:
(December 19)

*Galatians 6:7-10

"Do not be deceived: God cannot be mocked. A man reaps what he sows . . . Let us not become weary in doing good . . . *Therefore, as we have opportunity, let us do good to all people, especially those who are in the family of believers.*"

God has eyes in every place. We may think we are getting away with doing something against God's will, but He sees everything. Whatever we sow, we will reap. If we do badly, we will reap bad results. If we do well, we reap eternal life with God. God wants us to do good to *all* people; treating people like you want to be treated.

DAY 352:
(December 20)

*James 3:5-11

"The tongue is a small part of the body, but it makes great boast . . . The tongue is a fire, a world of evil among the parts of the body. It corrupts the whole body . . . *no human being can tame the tongue. It is a ruthless evil, full of deadly poison* . . . Out of the same mouth comes praises and cursing . . ."

Our tongue is the part of the body that can bring blessing or curses to us. We sometimes speak death to our own situations or others' circumstances. God wants us to speak life (blessing) to our circumstances or others' situations. Life and death lies in the power of the tongue. Let's ask God to help us tame our tongues.

DAY 353:
(December 21)

Ephesians 6:10-17

"Be strong in the Lord and His mighty power. Put on the full armor of God, so that you can take your stand against the devil's schemes. *For our struggles are not against flesh and blood, but against the . . . powers of this dark world and against the spiritual forces of evil in the heavenly realm . . . stand firm . . ."*

We must protect ourselves from the powers of the devil. We must arm ourselves with the word of God. God's word is our protection from the devil and his evil tricks. Every word of God is the truth, life, power, and strength. Prayer is very important in our Christian walk with God.

DAY 354:
(December 22)

John 14:1-7

"Do not let your heart be troubled. You believe in God; believe also in Me . . . Thomas said to Him, Lord, we don't know where You are going, so how can we know the way. *Jesus answered, I am the way and the truth and the life. No one comes to the Father except through Me . . .*"

Jesus explains to His disciples (and us) that He would be leaving, but also that He was preparing a place for them (us). This will be our eternal, heavenly home. If we believe in Jesus, then we also believe in God. God sent Jesus to dwell with us, to show (teach) us the way to everlasting life with God. We need to keep the faith and follow Jesus with all of our hearts, minds, and souls.

DAY 355:
(December 23)

Psalm 51:6-12

"Behold, You desire truth in the inward parts, and in the hidden parts You will make me to know wisdom . . . wash me, and I will be whiter than snow . . . Hide Your face from my sins . . . *Create in me a clean heart . . . renew a steadfast spirit within me . . .*"

David was pleading with God to renew and restore his heart, mind, and soul. He wanted to change his life in order to be pleasing to God. We ought to pray and ask God to create in us a clean heart and renew a right spirit within us.

DAY 356:
(December 24)

Psalm 139:23-24

"*Search me, God, and know my heart; test me and know my anxious thoughts. See if there is any offensive ways in me,* and lead me in the way of everlasting life."

David, the Psalmist, sinned against God and constantly pleaded to God for forgiveness. We ought to ask God to look into our hearts, minds, and souls to see if we have sinned against Him. We can say positive things from our mouths, but the intentions in our hearts are negative. Help us, Lord, to express genuine, pure love toward You and others. It is God's will for us to be like Jesus.

DAY 357:
(December 25)
MERRY CHRISTMAS

Isaiah 9:6-7

"For to us a Child is born, to us a Son is given, and the government will be on His shoulders. And He will be called Wonderful Counselor, Mighty God, Everlasting Father, Prince of Peace . . . He will reign on David's throne and over His kingdom . . . The zeal of the Lord Almighty will accomplish this."

We serve a Mighty God. He is the Great I Am, the Alpha and the Omega. He is the Beginning and the End, the First and the Last. There is no one above Him. Let's surrender our hearts, minds, and souls to Him as a living sacrifices. Today is a good day to repent, ask for forgiveness, and believe in the Lord Jesus Christ. Let's believe in our hearts that God sent His Son Jesus to die for our sins, confess with our mouth that Jesus is the Messiah, and repent and ask God to forgive us. Today is the beginning of the rest of our lives.

Christmas is a celebration of Jesus' birth. This season is not about presents (gifts), but the presence of Jesus in our lives. God asked me to tell His people that during this holiday, we should remember that Jesus is the reason for the season. Let's dedicate our lives to God as a living sacrifice, holy and acceptable to Him. What better gift than to give your life to Christ. It will be the best thing you have ever done in your life. God is waiting for us to prepare for having everlasting life with Him. God wants us to tell our children and our children's children about His birth. Let's celebrate this Christmas and every Christmas to come showing God how much we love Him.

*A **Christmas Prayer:** Lord, there are only a few more weeks before the end of this book. God, I made a commitment to write this book from December 31 until December 31,or 365 days. I first want to thank You, Lord, because without You I don't know how I could have made it this far. My prayer today is for revelation knowledge for my next assignment. Help me, Lord, to see, hear, and do what You would have for me do next. I trust You in every situation. Many individuals want to continue receiving the morning inspirations. I would be willing to continue with this divine assignment. I pray today that if you would have me do something else, someone will take over and continue sending these messages out to Your people. I give all the honor, glory, and praise to my Lord and Savior, Jesus Christ, Amen!*

DAY 358:
(December 26)

Mark 13:26-37

"*But about that day or hour no one knows, not even the angels in heaven*, nor the Son, but only the Father. Be on guard! Be alert! You do not know when that time will come."

The Bible says, Jesus will return like a thief in the night. He will come quickly, like a blink of an eye. We do not want to be caught sleeping or unprepared. We need to get our house in order now, so we can offer Him entrance. We want to be pleasing to God, loving and acceptable, teaching others about His goodness. Let's pray and ask God to help us be ready for His return.

DAY 359:
(December 27)

***1 Peter 3:13-17**

"Who is going to harm you if you are eager to do good? But even if you should suffer for what is right, you are blessed. Do not fear their threats, do not be frightened . . . *Always be prepared to give an answer to everyone who asks you to the reason for the hope that you have.*"

We will all suffer at one point in time. Jesus suffered and died for us; therefore, we must suffer also. These trials and challenges we go through are only to make us strong. When asked to tell about our hope, we only need to give our testimonies of how good God is.

DAY 360:
(December 28)

2 Corinthians 5:15-21

"And He died for all, that those who live should live no longer for themselves, but for Him . . . *Therefore, if anyone is in Christ, he is a new creation; old things have passed away, behold, all things have become new.*"

Christ became sin; although He never sinned; He suffered and died to take our sins away. We owe it to Him to surrender our lives to Him and serve Him with all of our beings. Being in Christ Jesus, we become new creations, our lives being devoted to serving Him.

DAY 361:
(December 29)

Hebrews 13:1-4

"Let brotherly love continue. *Do not forget to entertain strangers, for by so doing some have unwittingly entertained angels.* Remember the prisoners as if chained to them—those who are mistreated—since you yourselves are in the body also."

We must remember that we are all made in the image of God. We all belong to God, our Father. God wants us to treat one another with love, no matter what. We should treat each other with kindness at all times, because we never know who God will send into our lives to minister to us.

DAY 362:
(December 30)

Proverbs 3:1-6

"My son, do not forget My teaching, but keep My commandments in your heart, for they will prolong your life many years . . . *Trust in the Lord with all your heart and lean not to your own understanding,* in all your ways submit to Him, and He will make your paths straight.

We ought to put *all* of our trust in the Lord. He is the only One to help us when we cannot help ourselves. When our mother and father forsake us, then the Lord will take us up. We really cannot depend on anyone, except God. He is our Father, mother, doctor, and lawyer; He is our everything. Let's pray and ask God to help us follow His commandments and His will.

Psalm 30:4-6

"Sing praise to the Lord, you saints of His . . . For His anger is but for a moment, His favor is for life; *weeping may endure for a night, but joy comes in the morning.*"

We are all bound to go through some kinds of trials and tribulations. God has given us His promise that it won't last forever. After it's all said and done and the dust has settled, the joy of the Lord will cover us. Always trust the word of God.

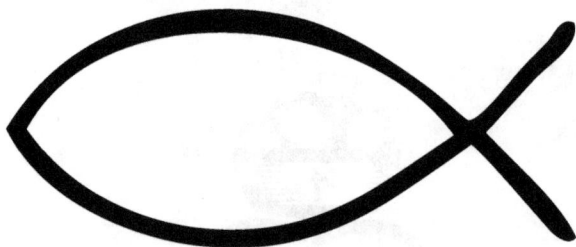

DAY 364:
(January 1)

Leviticus 19:11-18

"Do not steal. Do not lie. Do not deceive one another . . . Do not go about spreading slander among your people . . . *Do not seek revenge or bear a grudge against anyone among your people, but love your neighbor as yourself.*"

God has set His laws and decrees into place. He only asks that we follow them to the best of our ability. We need only to pray and ask God to help us follow His commandments and love one another. He will help us if and when we ask (pray).

DAY 365:
(January 2)

*Matthew 6:25-34

"Therefore I say to you, do not worry about your life, what you will eat or what you will drink; nor about your body, what you will put on . . . *But seek first the kingdom of God and His righteousness, and all these things shall be added to you. Therefore do not worry about tomorrow, for tomorrow will worry about its own things.*"

God has given us detailed instructions not to worry about the cares of this world. He promises that He will take care of our every need. He will make sure we have all of the human basic needs: food, clothes, water, shelter, and love. Let's lean on the promises of God to live this life.

Conclusion

This is the last entry to *Cooper's Morning Inspirations: A Spiritual Journey*. I cannot and will not end this book without acknowledging my mother, Patsy. She has been a very inspiring factor in my prayer life. My mother has been the backbone of my family for many years. I watched my mother go to the church to pray daily at 12:00 noon. I adopted that habit and have been practicing going to the church to pray daily. I came to live with my mother without two pennies to rub together. I came on Mother's Day, smiling, and told her that I was her gift for that year. She opened her home and her heart with unconditional love. I could always feel the presence of the Lord on her and in her home. I got saved in her house. (To read the complete story, get ready for my second book entitled *An Ordinary Man in an Ordinary World: A Spiritual Journey*. This book is in process and should be out soon.

This has truly been a spiritual journey. God has been accompanying me throughout this entire process. I made a commitment to God that I would write this book in the name of Jesus. The book would begin on December 31 and end on December 31 the following year. My mission is accomplished, and I believe God is pleased.

I would like to encourage my readers to activate the spiritual gifts God has given to each and every one of you. God wants us to press towards the prize of the upward call, which is in Christ Jesus. We must get involved with a local church community and work for the kingdom of God. If we pray, God will reveal which gift or area He wants us to work in. Everything we do for God, the church, and ourselves should be done in the name of Jesus.

I want to leave my readers with an encouraging presentation I gave at my church. I believe God wants us to become active in our church and continue to lead the unsaved to His house. He wants us to tell others about His goodness, His promises, and His unconditional love for all people.

ACTIVATE YOUR GIFTS

Philippians 3:13-15

"One thing I do, forgetting what is behind and reaching forward to what is ahead, I press on toward the goal for the prize of the upward call of God in Christ Jesus. Therefore let us, as many as are mature, have this mind; if in anything you think otherwise, God will reveal even this to you."

Activate Your Gifts

We are going to run into things that will seem to stop our progress, things have the tendency of coming from out of nowhere to disrupt us and knock us off balance.

We must first start with a *prayer life*. It is very important to stay in the presence of God. He is going to be our *ultimate help*. God do not want us to give up. He wants us to *keep reaching* toward *our* upward call.

1 Corinthians 12:4-14

"There are different kinds of gifts, but the same Spirit distributes them. There are different kinds of service, but the same Lord. There are different kinds of working, but in all of them and in everyone it is the same God at work."

Some might be *preachers, deacons, teachers,* and so forth, but *let God have His way.*

For in fact, the body is *not one member but many.*

My Gifts

When I got saved, *God* laid the *nursing home ministry* on my heart. I personally went out and pursued this myself. There were many things that tried to come against this, but I continued to *activate my gifts.*

The one thing I learned from God is to *continue to pray.* I stayed in the prayer room, on my face, as often as I was able. I continue to do this today.

A Mother's Note

This is a brief history of one of my sons. We lived in a small town called Cambridge, Maryland. Back then, we did not have much, but we made it. I had to pick crabs, skin tomatoes, and worked in couple of shirt factories. Since times were hard, I decided to move to Trenton, New Jersey. While living in New Jersey, my son hardly hung around his brothers and sisters. He didn't talk much and never got into any trouble. He spent most of his time, hanging with the pastor's son. I would call the church and the preacher would say: "He's okay, he's in the church." My son would stay at the church most of the day; sometimes all day long.

I think it is a blessing that God would use my son to write a devotional book. I believe it will help somebody, somewhere, get closer to God.

Love, Your Mother,

Patsy McNeil

("Mommo")

www.ingramcontent.com/pod-product-compliance
Lightning Source LLC
Chambersburg PA
CBHW062358090426
42740CB00010B/1323